Lines by Lines

Lines by Lines

Lyrical Works

Marian Lines

Matador
9 Priory Business Park
Kibworth Beauchamp
Leicestershire LE8 0RX, UK
Tel: (+44) 116 279 2299
Fax: (+44) 116 279 2277
Email: books@troubador.co.uk
Web: www.troubador.co.uk/matador

ISBN 978 1780884 677

British Library Cataloguing in Publication Data.
A catalogue record for this book is available from the British Library.

Typeset in the UK by Troubador Publishing Ltd
Printed and bound in the UK by TJ International, Padstow, Cornwall

Matador is an imprint of Troubador Publishing Ltd

For Betty, Iain and Robyn

AUTHOR'S NOTE

Writing lyrics to be set to music by a composer has always been the greatest pleasure imaginable to me.

I've been remarkably lucky to have worked for forty years with two women composers: Rosalind Roland 1969 – 1973, and Betty Roe MBE 1975 to the present.

Many early pieces were written for a drama club or choir because I wanted a song, cantata or musical which fitted the children's age and abilities, but most often commissions came through the late John Bishop, Betty's husband and music publisher, and his wide contacts in the music world. John also published Betty and my children's mini musicals.

A request for an opera, a song cycle or a musical play would arrive via a phone-call from John or Betty, and the whole exciting process would begin. A specific theme would usually be attached to the commission, and after offering a brief outline, scenario or taste of the atmosphere for approval, we would get started.

The words were written first on almost all occasions – Betty describes herself as a setter of words – and that's how we worked. I have always used the layout and groupings of the words, sometimes in verses - sometimes in broken lines straight across the page - to indicate emotion, humour, tempo, shape. The form of a number, or whole item, is how I try to communicate my ideas to the composer, and though this might appear a bit chaotic to a reader, it has largely worked.

Betty (and most songwriters or setters of lyrics) like some rhyme in the words, and an old, battered Thesaurus is my most prized companion. I write many lists of rhyming words on scraps of paper and search Roget for unexpected or odd rhymes. Often I can't find what I want and this forces me to turn the lyric inside-out and so come up with something much more interesting that I'd originally planned. I've never used a rhyming dictionary – though I have been tempted.

However... (dot dot dot, one of my favourite punctuation marks) all the work, drafting and music and theatre experience in the world cannot pacify the lyricist when, after a performance, an audience member says, "That was lovely! What a shame we couldn't hear all the words...".

Those unheard words are the reason for this collection.

CONTENTS

INTRODUCTION

It is difficult to recall a time when Marian's lyrics were not part of my home or professional life. As a child I clearly remember the envelopes from Marian thudding onto our doormat, to be set by my mum, Betty (and often returned the same day!). As a teenager, student and young professional I sang in and played for many of their hugely enjoyable musicals and choral pieces, including 'The Barnstormers', 'The Pink Parakeet', 'Pardon Our Rubbish' (with an environmental theme years ahead of its time) and 'Most Wanted Faces'. Later came community and intergenerational productions like 'Crowds', 'Christmas Boxes' and 'The Family Tree'. One of my most treasured memories is of my own two children performing in the panto extravaganza 'Dick Whittington' – 15+ years later we still have the costumes and they remember all their lines!

Marian's crisp, well-paced, often highly humorous scripts and lyrics were a treat but it was only as my own school-based teaching life began to develop during the 1990s that I began to appreciate Marian's literary skills, particularly when writing for children. The Lines / Roe production line proved to be a lifesaver as I searched for suitable resources to present to pupils from an ever wider range of abilities, backgrounds and experience. Time and time again I came back to these productions, which always worked brilliantly in a variety of settings and circumstances.

I was frequently disappointed by the parlous standard of much material promoted for children, which either seemed aimed for those at 'chorister' level or combined the very worst elements of musical pastiche with lyrics that were unimaginative, simplistic and clumsy. Scripts were often weak with characters poorly defined and under developed. So what a relief just to read one of Marian's fabulously irreverent cast lists, such as that from 'Most Wanted Faces' or 'The Barnstormers', evocative names followed by a brief, punchy character description, which instantly captures the core and driving force of each distinct personality.

Marian uses sophisticated language and her texts have a strong but natural rhythmic flow - no surprise as she possesses a beautiful singing voice. She is lean with words, with not a wasted syllable. Marian never 'talks down', assuming (quite rightly) that young people instinctively understand far more about the subtleties of life and the challenges presented by human nature than adults are inclined to give them credit for. She is able to explore and successfully address complicated events and emotions (as in 'Crowds') and present complex, sometimes sinister characters that nevertheless ring true, like Madame Rosa from 'The Pink Parakeet' and the largely feline, mysterious cast of 'The Cat's Tale'.

Perhaps more than anything else, Marian's lyrics demonstrate her enormous capacity for fun, to generate and enjoy laughter. Her work is peppered with humour, both through the characters she creates and by the situations she presents. In 'The Barnstormers', Marian's use of the 'play within a play' is brilliant, as Theo Trouncer, playing 'Squire Squeeze', becomes more and more confused, almost causing his poor prompt Frisby to suffer a cardiac arrest! An audience recognises Marian's characters and is drawn to them, cares about them, wants to know what happens next and is sorry to see them go.

In this new twitter-fed world, Marian's work reminds us that a well-chosen word or phrase can often create a touch of magic.

Soo Bishop
August 2012

SONGS

3 SONGS FOR BARITONE
Written for Graham Trew, 2010

The Promising Gardener

Tomorrow I shall dig the left-hand bed…
And hoe the weeds
And prune the apricot –
Unless I lop that rotten branch instead,
Or move the rose beside the bergamot…?
       Yes – I'll see to that tomorrow.

Of course, we'll have to hope the weather's fine,
There's not much sense
In digging in the rain…
And if I don't cut down the Russian Vine
I'll have to nail that trellis up again.
       Mmm – I'll work that out tomorrow.

From here, inside, the daffodils look good…
And hyacinths,
Crocus and snowdrops too.
I ought to get out there, I really should;
Now Spring is sprung there's such a lot to do.
       Right – all set for tomorrow!

Let's see what Ceefax says about the weather…
Ooh…'gale-force winds'…
The forecast, 'wet and bleak'!
Well, that's put paid to gardening altogether;
I'll have to put it off until next week.
       Still – it's a shame about tomorrow;
       I was looking forward to a little gardening.

The Dream House

It came in a dream –
A house on a green hill,
Round like a tower,
Round like a windmill.
He woke in the night,
Woke in the night chill;
Knew he must live
In a house like a windmill.

So he builded his house
High on a green hill,
It was round like a tower,
Round like a windmill;
And his friends came up,
Up to the green hill,
To the house like a tower
That was round like a windmill.

Then the wine went round
Till they had drunk their fill,
And the talk went round and round
Like the sails of a windmill.

Now the years have gone round,
Yet he lives there still,
In the round house,
Like a round tower
On the green, green hill.

Scooting

I was standing at the bus-stop
Thinking, 'surely *something* must stop,
Can they *all* be making for the terminus?'
When I heard a little voice
Piping, 'well, you've got a choice;
You'd be better off employing one of us'.

I looked round in blank amazement,
When I noticed on the pavement
Where a silver scooter leant against the wall.
So I dashed into a store,
Selling scooters by the score,
And bought the most expensive one of all.

And...I... go... scoot, scoot, scooting on my scooter,
Through city streets and up the mountainside;
And no-one would dispute
That there's anything as cute
As seeing me scoot-scooting in me pride.

T'was a life-transforming moment
By that bus-stop on the pavement;
I've escaped the queues and cars I can't abide.
No more honking, no more hooting,
No more hairy red-light-shooting,
Life is on a different footing,
I'm the Emperor of Scooting...
With my trusty little scooter by my side!

from **TOWER BLOCKS**
Written for the children of Fox School and published by
Franklyn Watts in 1974

Fairground

Organ-shout music, kaleidoscope streamers,
Big-Dipper hooters and Dodge-'Em Car screamers,
Roundabout motors and buses and steamers,
"Walk up, folks....
"Walk up, folks, come to the......"

Ear-splitting shooting range, trot-trotting donkeys,
Blue and red cockatoos, clambering monkeys,
Crowd noises, loud noises, shrill honky-tonkies,
"Walk up, folks....
"Walk up, folks, come to the......"

Gypsy magicians and goldfish for prizes,
Candy-floss sugar in gigantic sizes,
Heart-stopping Ghost Train with screeching surprises,
"Walk up, folks....
"Walk up, folks, come to the Fair! Come to the Fair!"

Tower Block

How did I come to be here in the sky?...
Twenty-five storeys above you am I,
With the pavement so low, below.....
                           Wind singing to and fro.

I once had a dream that I wanted to fly,
Over pavements so low below,
Now twenty-five storeys above you am I...
                           Wind singing to and fro.

How did I come to be living so high?....
Twenty-five storeys above you am I,
With the pavement so far below......
                           Tower block swings to and fro.

MEN WERE DECEIVERS EVER
Commissioned in 1978

Love's Gluttony

To fair Clarissa how my heart doth cleave
To dear Melissa now my heart I leave
While Clara-Ann and Melisande
Hold each one part of my torn heart
And toss it here and there
And fling it in the air
So is my poor tormented heart a wreck
At every beauteous maiden's call and beck
Call, beck, beck, call, call and beck, beck and call.
Oh, bloomin' 'eck
I'd like to chuck it all.

When sweetest Meg in silken dalliance plays
When buxom Peg beguiles with winning ways
When Lillian and Gillian
Combine with ease to tease and please
And lead me up and down
'Twixt every smile and frown
Then is my manhood hookèd like a fish
As these fair maids indulge each whim and wish,
Whim, wish, wish, whim, whim and wish, wish and whim
Oh tush and pish, tush and pish, tush, pish and tush and pish
I'm feeling pretty grim

But now I mind me where this feast doth lead
And how these tempting dishes swell my greed!
So, so at last I needs must rest
Lest each new dox doth me intox
And land me on my back
Like some poor hap-less Jack.
These jolly wenches tumble to and fro
Till my survival's merely touch and go
Touch go, go touch, touch and go, go and touch
Oh pox on love, oh pox on, pox on, pox on love
I've wenched it wenched it far too much.

Home Sweet...

If you looked at me as I stood in church,
With my offspring ranged by my side
You would see a man, a family man
Aglow with familial pride.
Oh, you'd never glean from my sober mien
What a cauldron of passion boils deep down inside
For I walk the tight rope
The double-life tight rope,
I walk the tight rope from side to side.

If you looked at me as I sat at meat
With my offspring ranged round the board,
You would see a man, a family man,
A paterfamilial lord.
Oh, you'd little guess from my sober dress
What a whirlwind of passion about me roared
For I've trod the knife edge
The double-life knife edge
I've trod the knife edge but never been scored.

If you looked at me as I ran my mills,
When I lead my workforce in prayer,
You would see a man, an industrial man
With a firm magnanimous air.
Oh you'd little sense from my gaze intense
What a torrent of passion surges here
For I've juggled my eggshells,
My double life eggshells,
I've juggled my eggshells with consummate care!

If you looked at me as I took my ease
In a boudoir of plush and gold,
You would see a man, a two-faced man
With an eye both bright and bold.
You'd be bound to see from the girl on my knee
That I'm cast in the grand Casanovian mould
And I'll relish my knife edge –
Double-life knife edge –
My hell raising double-life till I'm cold!

The Business End of Love

My dearest, darling Egg-Foo-Young
Why do we have to wait so long
Before we manage to complete
The business started on the seat
Of your ex-husband's custom-built
(Power-steering trimmed with chrome and gilt)
White limousine with cocktail bar
(A really super-smashing car).
The fifteenth inst. has come and gone
But not my Yummy Egg-Foo-Young.

My Dear Miss Young I got your note
So sad about your putrid throat!
The grass was wet last Saturday
As for the crab I couldn't say –
I don't remember anything
(A little rash that fourth gin sling?)
Wrong with champagne and caviar
(I think perhaps you went too far?)
So sorry Thursday isn't on
But get well soon my dear Miss Young.

Dear Madam,
Since you think it best
To give our Wednesday nights a rest
Perhaps the end of March next year
As you suggest is rather near.
My time is not my own these days
(And rushing business never pays)
Perhaps some day we'll meet again...
My best regards to you till then.

Thank you Miss Jackson...
When you're clear
File under "Young"
And come in here!

CANTATAS

from **THE STORM HOUND**
commissioned by Gordon Pullin for the choir of Old Buckenham Hall, 1996

One August Sunday in 1577 a catastrophic storm struck the Suffolk village of Blythborough, destroying the church and killing many of the congregation. Black Shuck, the legendary Demon Hound was blamed.

Narrator/ Black Shuck
"All you who come to listen here today / Attend and hearken to my words, I pray.
I have a grim and grisly tale to tell / And you'll be witness that my tale wags well!

If you admire my fine, Italian style / My honeyed compliments, my ready smile,
Never forget the shade that dogs your dream / Beware of me – I am not what I seem!

Since angels fell, and Eden's gate was shut / Upon the foolish Adam and his slut;
Since men first settled on this shifting shore / Still have I hounded them with ravening maw.

Here Adam lived, in pitiful estate / I followed after, joying in his fate,
And took whatever fearful shape I might / Adding more terror to his soul's affright.

Black Shuck! With burning eyes and muzzle fell / With bellowing havoc and with quake from hell;
Compound of thun'drous tempest, fire and sea / Few can escape who walk the path with me!

Who mauls the coastline, drowning tree and town? / Worries the
sandbank, chews the cliff-rock down?
Swallowing Dunwich at the waves command / And stranding little
Beccles far inland?

So centuries of centuries have passed / And still my fateful footsteps
follow fast.
Frighting the timid, savaging the brave / Tempting the child to swim
the angry wave.

But I reserve my direst rage and spite / For those who worship in
the fair sunlight.
So smote I Blythburgh church from font to spire / Then Bungay's
parish felt my bitter ire.

I am a thing of legend – of nightmare / These fools will tell you
what you have to fear!"

Landlord & patrons of The Flower in Hand – Aldburgh
"Suffolk ale! Suffolk ale! Let's drink a toast to Suffolk Ale!
From Blythburgh to Hadleigh dale, we'll draw a jug of Suffolk ale!
Come in! Come in! Good neighbours come within.
Shut fast the door on snow and sleet, then share a bowl and take a seat
To warm your frozen hands and feet. Come in! Come in! Come in!
Tell us a tale! Tell us a tale! Tell us the terrible Blythborough tale!
Don't any know the mystery of that fatality?

And you, good sirs, whoe're you be, a' sitting there so quietly
In sad and silent secrecy – have you the truth for we?
Pray, don't look down and steal away,
But tell us straight what passed that day."

3 Blythborough men
"We were there in the church that Sunday morn,
Bright August, forty years a'gone.
The sun in glory smiled and beamed:
A fairer day was never seen.

We boys lay sprawled on oaken seat
To yawn and fret in summer heat;
And as I gazed through lofty glass
A glinting, silver flash do pass.
Then see I, through the crystal clear,
A black cloud like an omen there.

While parson drones and people sighs,
I glance outside with heavy eyes,
And see an inky menace there –
A cloud-tower in the bright blue air;
Then as we kneel in prayer, a gust
Flings wide the door with hammer-blast!
Black storm-clouds boil across the sun -
And into midnight we are thrown!

A thunderbolt, with clamorous clap
Splits wide the roof, with horrid hap!
Such thunder, lightning, rain and hail
That teemeth down on tempest gale,
Belab'ring us with wicked whips
Seems herald to th'Apocolypse!
Now clap on clap our eardrums split
As darkness is by lightning lit.

Now fireballs flame the choir stalls,
Now like the deluge torrents fall.
The people scream – they cower or run,
Cry, 'Armageddon is begun… begun!'
When thund'rously the church door slams,
And through the roof The Horror comes!
Down through the roof The Horror comes!

The Storm Hound, sent from Satan's Halls,
Upon the congregation falls!
Black as the night, with gaping jaw,

With flaring eye and bloody maw,
The Monster leaps with baying howl,
With scourging claw and fiendish growl!
Compound of evil, darkness, death,
With razor teeth and brimstone breath,
He mauls and worries, bites and burns –
Then on the next poor soul he turns!
The abject people shriek with fear,
'Beware! Beware! The Devil's here!'
Then to the church roof leaps The Hound,
Tumbling the spire to the ground;
Thunders upon his devilish path
Borne onwards by the wings of wrath:
Leaving a carnage-tainted smirch
Upon the shell of Blythborough church.
We living stared in unbelief,
With glazèd eyes and smothered grief,
On sights of fire, death and flood
Where once a place of worship stood.

The sun once more in glory beamed,
A fairer day was never seen.
God's mercy now we pray,
For them that died that day.
The sights we saw at Blythborough then
Turned carefree boys to blighted men.

"Let's drink a solemn toast to them, once carefree boys, now blighted men.
Suffolk ale! Suffolk ale! Let's drink a toast to Suffolk Ale!
From Blythburgh to Hadleigh ale, we'll drink a toast in Suffolk ale!"

For this time, truly, you have heard the sound
The fateful footsteps of BLACK SHUCK –
THE STORM HOUND!

from **A CAT'S TALE**
commissioned by Ronald Corp for the Finchley Children's Music Group, published in 1990

On a cold winter afternoon, schoolchildren tiptoe past the churchyard, scared by the sound of digging. The Sexton is alarmed too, and rushes home with a dark tale for his wife – but his tomcat is delighted!

Schoolchildren
By a dark, dark hill / Down a dark, dark lane / Past the dark, dark trees / Stands a little dark church

When we walk home from school on a cold winter's night
With our hearts in our boots and our breath ghostly white,
How we shiver and shake as we steal down the lane.
  Do you hear what I hear?
  There it goes again!
  Somebody's digging a grave...
So we creep through the hedge by the little church wall,
And what do we see? Why, no one at all,
But the digging gets louder though we cannot see where;
  Then a voice begins singing...
  Do you hear what I hear?
  Crick, crack, crick crack!
  What's that, what's that?
With a snick and a snack and a knucklebone crack,
  Somebody's digging a grave!
Oh, somebody's shovelling, digging and shovelling
  Somebody's digging a grave!

Sexton
A'digging and a'delving down deep in the earth;
A'down six feet under the grass and the turf –
It's stony and bony, it's dark and it's drear,

Makes you shiver with ague at this time of year...
  But it's jolly, yes, jolly in a grim kind of way
  To be down six feet under on a dark winter's day.
  A'digging and a'delving, a'delving and a'digging
  A'digging and a'delving on a dark winter's day.

  A'shovelling and a'scraping from morning till night;
  A'scrabbling about till there ain't no more light.
  It's dark and it's chillsome, it's musty and sour –
  Makes you shudder with terror at this ghostly hour...

Old Mother Chumley to Heaven she hied;
She turned up her toes and she lay down and died.
Now up with the Angels she's flying around,
While I'm in this bone-yard, six feet underground...
  But it's jolly, yes, jolly in a grim kind of way
  To be down six feet under on a dark winter's day.
  A'digging and a'delving, a'delving and a'digging
  A'digging and a'delving on a dark winter's day.

Hey! Ho! Who's up there? All you little children better beware!
Get home to your teas as fast as you can, or I'll send for the bony old
Bogey-Man!
Run! Run as fast as you can! You've got to get away from the
Bogey-Man!

Sexton's wife
In the Sexton's cottage, all warm and cosy,
The Sexton's wife, all round and rosy.
Nice old armchair, comfy-wide,
Tom cat curled by the snug fireside.
Bubbling kettle, warming pot,
Toast well buttered and steaming hot.
Knitting-needles click in the fireside's glow,
While the good-wife's chair rocks to-and-fro.

I sing as I knit and I knit as I sing / In praise of Tom… My cat Tom.
Dear Tom, sweet Tom / Demure and neat Tom;
Good Tom, meek Tom / Furry, sleek Tom;
Purr, Tom, nap Tom / Sit on my lap, Tom.
Play, Tom, bounce Tom / Hunt and pounce, Tom.
Tom by the fireside, Tom on the mat,
What can compare to our own Tom Cat.

Then in through the door / With a crash and a roar / Face like chalk
Scarce able to walk,
Teeth a'chatter / Feet a'clatter / Chatter, chatter, clatter, clatter /
Quaking with fear jumps the Sexton!

Wife
Oh, husband what's amiss, what's amiss, what's amiss?
Won't you tell me what has happened? / Won't you tell me
what's the matter?
Oh, I've never seen you look like this, my dear / I've never seen
you look like this!

Sexton
Oh, wife, oh, wife, I have seen such a sight / I shall never forget
this dreadful night!
Now listen to the tale I tell, my dear / Listen to the tale I tell…

His cat sits up
His wife sits down
Ears all pricked,
Eyes all round.

Sexton
I was digging and a'delving down deep in the earth;
A'down six feet under the grass and the turf.
When all of a sudden I hears this strange knell,
Like the sound of a miniature funeral bell!
I peeped o'er the edge and what did I spy?
Seven little pussy-cats pacing by!

23

With bell, and coffin, and mournful cry,
They miaowed as they paced so slowly by.
Then what do I see as I poke and I pry -
On the little willow coffin passing by -
A little gold crown on a velvet mat.
And the mourners mewing for 'Old King Cat'!

Sang: "Old King Cat is dead / The King is dead.
King Cat lies in his little willow casket,
No cat sleeps in his fireside basket,
He ruled us well for seven years long,
Now his funeral bell rings 'Dong, ding-dong',
For Old King Cat is dead!"

Wife
Why, look at our puss-cat, hair on end! / Lawks a-mussy-me and
Heaven defend!
What's the matter with the cat? / What's the matter with Tom?
He's twice his size / He's fat as he's long!
Oh, whatever is the matter with Tom, my dear? / Whatever is the
matter with Tom?

Tom Cat
I can hardly believe the news I hear,
The news that I've waited for this long year!
Ah, what a wonder – me oh my,
I'm ready to burst, I'm ready to fly!

Oh, I've waited and waited and bided my time,
And I've dreamt and I've dreamt that the crown would be mine.
Then all of a sudden, at midnight last week
I woke to the sound of the King Cat's last shriek!

For I felt it in my whiskers and I felt it in my claws,
From the tip of my tail to the pads of my paws!
From my shiny black coat to my snowy white spats –
I *knew* I was born to the KING of the CATS!

from **ASTRON**

commissioned by Coloma School, Croydon, published in 1994

The year is 2900. On the artificial planet ASTRON, a crucial political ceremony is in mid-session when a small inter-galactic spacecraft – Cradle Two - crash-lands with its cargo of refugees. They are interrogated.

> *Yeggmon*
> Yeggmon's the name,
> Captain Yeggmon;
> Man of the purse,
> That's my game!
> Yeggmon's the name,
> Varlet Yeggmon,
> Lifting the loot,
> That's my aim.
>
> > Draining the rich ones dry,
> > Picking the rich ones bare:
> > Plucking the rich ones bald,
> > Nothing I dare not dare!
>
> Slapping the fat-cats down,
> Pricking the fat-cat's pride,
> Pulling the fat-cat's tail,
> Nothing I haven't tried!
>
> Singeing the fat-cat's fur,
> Cutting the fat-cat's claws,
> Stealing the fat-cat's mouse,
> Out of the fat-cat's jaws!

But on the other hand...
Helping the truant run,
Bringing the outcast back,
Smuggling the exiles home,
Hiding the outlaw's track!

>Want a cheap ride?
>Ask for Yeggmon.
>Find you a snug
>Place to hide.
>Dodging the war?
>Yeggmon's trusty
>Get you out fast –
>Past the law!

Yes – Yeggmon's the name!

Minna
I was going home / Wanted to get home / Needed to get home
Had to hurry home / Booked my passage home / Dying to get home
Home to Sagittarius.

Husband was at home / Family at home / Waiting there at home
Begged me to come home / Wanting me at home / Safely there at home
Home in Sagittarius.

But my baby, my baby, my baby wouldn't wait
Wanted me to see him / Wanted me to hold him / Wanted me to carry him
Home to Sagittarius.

And now we're far from home / May not get back home / Husband waits at home
Dying to get home / Won't you guide us home? / Help us to get home?
Home to Sagittarius?

Frondoro
I will fight and die – for Freedom!
I will hide, or fly – for Freedom!
Give my final breath, risk a martyr's death –
For Freedom!

Once upon a time my land was free,
Simple things were sweet,
Now the people live in slavery,
Shackles on their feet.

So...
Kept my country's faith,
Braved th'oppressors wrath
For Freedom!

Kludge
Kludge of the engine-room, that's me

I've a fondness for flywheels / A real love of levers
A weakness for wrenches / And partial to pistons.
I've a thing about throttles / I crave carburettors
Go soppy for spark-plugs / Have a kindness for klaxons...
(*blare of horns*)
Whoo hoo hoo ooh! Stop it!

When I'm up to me ears in oil,
And the boiler starts to boil.
When the circuits on the blink,
Or the pressure starts to sink.
When the air-locks gone for broke,
Or "Safety First"'s a joke;
When the fire-alarm is screaming,
And the cooling-system's steaming,
When "Abandon Ship"'s the shout,
When they're howling to get out...

Don't panic –
Call for Kludge!

I'm attracted to axles / Mad about manifolds
Crazy for crankshafts / A fan of the fanbelt
Transported by transport / Wowed by the welding.
Swoon over sprockets / Aaaah! Machines make my heart melt.

(Mind you, I couldn't do much when your gravity grabbed us.)

Soooooo…
When you're fearing the worst / And your boiler is burst…
Don't panic –
Call for Kludge!

CHORAL
FANTASIES

A RECIPE FOR GINGERBREAD
Commissioned for the Petersfield Festival, 1998

* ★ Plain flour, three quarters of a pound
* ★ Salt, half a teaspoon
* ★ Ginger, one small desert spoon
* ★ Butter, three ounces
* ★ Soft brown sugar, two ounces
* ★ Golden syrup, three ounces
* ★ Two medium eggs

Bake a batch of Ginger biscuits
Brew a butt of Ginger wine
Ginger candy, cakes and brandy;
Sugar and spice and all things fine.

Once on a time lived Grandma, Grandpa.
Lived in a cottage down in Peter's Field.
Little thatched roof and vine round the doorway.
Lavender path into Peter's Field.

Down in Peter's grassy field
Where daisies star with gold and green
Where Jack and Jill weave daisy chains
In Peter's green and grassy field.

Grandpa was grumpy, Grandpa was sad.
He wanted some cookies and wanted them bad.
He moaned and he groaned; "This is making me sick,
I've got to have biscuits, so bake me some quick."

Gingerbread for you, Gingerbread for me
Put it on a china plate and serve it for my tea.

* Plain flour, three quarters of a pound
* Salt, half a teaspoon
* Ginger, one small desert spoon
* Butter, three ounces
* Soft brown sugar, two ounces
* Golden syrup, three ounces
* Two medium eggs

Grandma
Grandma's baking
Grandma's baking gingerbread
Grandma's baking a Gingerbread Baby

Mixing and rolling and cutting and crimping
With currants for buttons and raisins for eyes.
Sugar and spice for fingers and toes…
Open the oven and in it goes.

Grandma's nodding,
The rocking chair's rocking
The clock is tick-tocking
And Grandma is nodding
Tick-tocking, tick-tocking
The clock is tick-tocking
While Grandmother nods
And the rocking chair rocks.

There's a sweet spicy smell from the oven.
There's a sweet spicy smell in the air.
It weaves like a charm through the window,
To Grandfather digging out there.

There's a knock-knock-knock from the oven,
But Grandma's asleep in her chair,
Then, three-four-open-the-door
And the Gingerbread Baby is here.

Up jumps Grandma
Brisk as a bee
"Gingerbread Baby
Come here to me!
Fetch me a knife,
A saucer and a cup,
Then hop on my plate
And I'll gobble you up!"

But the Baby's too quick for the lady
It's *far* too quick for the lady
"Run, run, run as fast as maybe
You can't catch me, I'm a Gingerbread Baby!"

Grandmother, Grandmother!
Where has it gone?
A skip and a hop
And away it has run!
With a skip and a hop and a hop and a skip
It's escaped from your kitchen, Grandmother!

Through garden it hops and a skips
Bumps into Grandpa hoeing the turnips
"Gingerbread Baby, where are you off to?
You're my special treat and I'm going to eat you!"

"Run, run, run as fast as maybe
You can't catch me, I'm a Gingerbread Baby!"

Humming honey summer bees
Which tread the pollen-heavy bloom
And hoard in nectar-scented wax
A luscious load of honeycomb.

Half asleep and half awake
At tranquil ease dream Jack and Jill
Among the nodding poppy heads
That fringe the corn by Butser Hill.

When up the lane like a little steam train
Comes the Gingerbread Baby on runaway wheels;
With a whoop and a hop, like a top that won't stop
And Grandma and Grandpa hot on his heels.

Jack and Jill feel famished as they watch the Gingerbread race
Jack and Jill run down the hill to join the Gingerbread chase.

But the Gingerbread Baby it never looks back
Like a little steam train on a railway track,
It sings and it whistles as loud as can be
"You can run if you like but you can't catch me!"

"Run, run, run as fast as maybe
You can't catch me, I'm a Gingerbread Baby!"

Swiftly past Steep
Faster by Foxfield
Hopped to High Cross
Pranced through Privett
Lingered at Langrish
Rambled round Ramsdean
Skipped into Stroud
Wandered up to Weston
Edged into East Meon
Bounced up Butser Hill
Walked across Watdown
Loitered at Liss
Ran into Rake
Hastened by Hawkley
Puffed into Petersfield
Shambled to Sleet

Rolled about Rogate
Trotted through Tretton
Nipped into Nywood
Blundered past Buriton
Nimbled over Nurstead
Halted at Harting - East *and* South
Then on, on to Beaston and Cocking
Till it came to the River Rother.
Tongue twisting frothing and foaming along
And it couldn't get across!

At the waterside
Sat Ferryman Fox
With red bushy tail
And black fur socks
A nose like a "V"
A grin like a trap
Sat Ferryman Fox
In his black fur socks.

"You've been running away
For nearly a day
Can I give you a lift?"
Smiled Ferryman Fox
"Jump on my tail
Like a Gingerbread sail
And I'll get you across."
Said Ferryman Fox.

So they plunged into the River Rother leaving Grandma, Grandpa,
Jack and Jill boo-hooing on the bank, but the Fox's tail began to
sink.

"Swim! swim! as fast as maybe
I mustn't get wet, I'm a Gingerbread Baby!"

"Jump on my back
You'll soon get the knack"
Smiled Ferryman Fox
In his swimming socks.

But soon the water was lapping over the Fox's back and the Baby
shouted...

"Swim! swim! as fast as maybe
I mustn't get wet, I'm a Gingerbread Baby!"

"Jump on my head,
It's dead easy", he said
With a grin and a wink,
"That part's *bound* not to sink!"

But the water it rose and it rose and it rose
And it rose right up to the Ferryman's nose.

"Swim! swim! as fast as maybe
I mustn't get wet, I'm a Gingerbread Baby!"

"Jump on my nose,
If I keep my mouth closed
You'll be safe as a ...

Crunch, crunch, munch and crunch
The Fox is enjoying his Gingerbread lunch!

The Moral:
        Though at running
You may be a Gingerbread winner...
You still may end up
As the Ferryman's dinner!

Snip, snap, snover –
        Another story's over ...

THE FAMILY TREE

Commissioned by Totteridge WI choir, for their diamond Jubilee,
1982

Upon this island stands a tree,
As full of branches as can be;
And every branch puts forth its leaves,
Its buds, its fruit, its blossom wreathes:
Nor hand can touch, nor eye can see
This tree that grows invisibly
And flourished full fruitfully –
This tree of human family.

Deep in the seed sleeps the tree...
Waits for its hour to be free,
Waits for the shoot,
Waits for the bud,
Waits for the flower,
Waits for its hour to be free.
Deep in the seed sleeps the tree...

Oh, the Family Tree, the Family Tree is sure to grow.
If we hadn't got a Family Tree we'd have passed on long ago.
Oh, a root-and-a-root and a shoot-and-a-shoot,
Some branches more or less;
If you meddle around with the Family Tree
You'll land up in a mess!

Oh, the Family Tree, the Family Tree has sprouts galore!
If you try to cut down the Family Tree you'll likely break the saw.
Oh, a blossom-a-blossom, a petal-a-petal,
Some foliage here and there;
If you meddle about with the Family Tree
You'll land up God knows where!

Oh, the Family Tree, the Family Tree goes on and on.

We'll never desert the Family Tree or the branch where we belong.

Oh, a bud and-a-bud and a seed-and-a-seed,

A flower, a fruit, a stone.

Don't meddle about with the Family Tree,

It's better left alone!

from **CHELSEA BALLET**

A ballet with spoken narrative commissioned by Thelma Bousefield, for the 1995 Chelsea Festival.

1950s, Chelsea Embankment. A shooting star lands on the statue of Sir Thomas More and wakes him to life. Wandering the riverside he is dumbfounded by the modern world.

Policeman (random phrases spoken in any order)
Copper at large
Walking his beat
Planting his ponderous feet
'Wot 'ave we 'ere?'
'Hullo, ullo'
'Hullo, and wot 'ave we 'ere?'
'Must write it down'
'Now:'…
"Proceedin' along the street"
"In an Easterly direction"
"7.00 AM"
"On the 2nd of May"
"As I approached
"Noted the fact"
"Sir Thomas's statue 'ad gone!"
"Seemed 'e'd vacated 'is chair"
"Must 'ave bin pinched"
"Pardon the phrase"
"Gotta make a report"
"Quite an event"
"Can't 'ave walked off all by 'imself"
"Don't know what the Sarge will make of it"
"Will make of this 'ere!"

Lovers

Meet me at the Albert Bridge
Say you love me…
Say you love me too…
Tell me that you…
Cross your heart and promise…
Promise that you'll never let me…
Never let me go…
That you'll never go!
Never ever let me go
Promise that you'll…
That you'll never…
Promise that…
Promise…
Never ever…
Won't let me…
Promise…
Promise…

Poodles & Their Owners

Oodles of Poodles –
    Powder and Pom-pom –
Doodley Noodles –
    Dandies of Dogdom –
Perfumed and Clippered –
    Diamante Collared –
Pampered and Slippered –
    Pounded and Dollared –
Fancy Dogs in Fancy Togs –
    Whenever they Pee –
Do it Delicately –
    [Don't Do it on Me!]
Frills and Bows and Furbelows
    And Puttees of Fluff are
Orange and Blue –
    Toodle-oo To You Too!
POODLES!

DICK WHITTINGTON

A pantomime

from **DICK WHITTINGTON**

Written for the Ladbroke Players and North Ken Chorale, 1995

A variation on the traditional story. After falling for Alice Fitzwarren, Dick sails off to seek his fortune, meeting adventures on the high seas and foreign lands, accompanied by Fairy Bow-Bells and King Rat.

Cap'n Bags-Oi
Whoi am Oi called 'Bags-Oi? / That's hobvious / Oi say,
'bags-Oi the the best 'ammock'
Or 'bags-Oi the laarst Fish Finger' / Or even 'bags-Oi most
of the treasure!'

With an 'Aaar!' an' an 'Eeee!'
And a 'Fiddle-de-de!'
Oi'm Cap'n Bags-Oi
That's me!

> Oi'm……..
> A rollicking son of the o-she-un wave,
> With a First Mate an' cabin-boy too.
> Oi've……..
> A cat-o-nine-tails to make 'em be'ave,
> The murderous, mutinous crew!
> Oi've……..
> A peg on me leg an' a pipe in me mouth;
> Oi rant an' Oi rave an' Oi roar!
> Oi'll………
> Shiver their timbers to North an' to South,
> Then Oi rants and Oi raves a bit more.

On..........
The blue rolling main moi ship is the best!
Though I found her just floating about.
She.........
Goes by the name of 'The Marie Celeste' –
They don't call me 'Bags-Oi' for nowt!
So..........
Hoist up the mains'l and break out the rum;
Give the crows-nest a jolly good scrub.
Bid.........
A tearful farewell to your grey-haired old Mum,
For we're off to the rub-a-dub-dub!

With an 'Aaar!' an' an 'Eeee!'
And a 'Fiddle-de-de!'
Oi'm Cap'n Bags-Oi
That's me!

Lady Shanghai
I'm Lady Shanghai,
I'm the Queen of the sea,
A rip-roaring buccaneer rover;
And flying aloft,
Why the first thing you see
Is my trade-mark,
The Jolly Old Roger!

I'll capture you all
In a hand-to-hand fight!
I'll scupper and scuttle
And spank you!
Your treasure is mine
By the privateer's right,
And a walk on the plank
Is my 'thank you'!

44

With an 'oo!' and an 'ah!'
And a 'ha, ha, ha!'
I'm Lady Shanghai
Yes, I am!

Cookie
They're always after me to cook something up for them!
It's 'Cookie!' this and
'Cookie!' that till I'm all of a dooh-dah! / It's...

'Cook – Cook – Cook –Cookie!
Cook a crumby cake for me!
Cook – Cook – Cook –Cookie!
Just in time for tea!
Your buns and baps are beautiful,
Your flans and flapjacks fruitful;
So -'Cook – Cook – Cook – Cookie!
Cook a crumby cake for me!'

They call me the Queen of the cookery-cooks –
Poor Nigella hasn't a chance!
For talent, for figure, for sparkle, for looks
I beat her, hands-down on all fronts!
She'll come round at midnight with, 'Lend us an egg?' –
For sugar she'll bang on my door.
There's always *some* thing she must borrow or beg
Till I tell 'er, 'Nigella... No more!'

Then I go back to bed once again,
Till I wake to this haunting refrain...'

'Cook – Cook – Cook –Cookie!
Cook a crumby cake for me!'
They're all of 'em after me strawberry pud –
That Ramsey won't let me alone.
I say to 'im, 'Gordon, your puddings are crud,
So kindly get off of me phone!'

They pester me here and they pester me there,
They ring and they write and they fax!
They beg on their knees for me Chicken Surprees
And they swoon for me dips and me snacks!

Those Brothers Roux are a real nuisance / They give me no
peace! / Chasing after me for me coulis, me butters, me
sauces / They're insatiable!

When I think that they've all gone away...
I'm bound to hear some beggar say...'
'Cook – Cook – Cook –Cookie!
Cook a crumby cake for me!
'Cook – Cook – Cook –Cookie!
Just in time for tea!
Your buns and baps are beautiful,
Your flans and flapjacks fruitiful,
Oh...
'Cook – Cook – Cook –Cookie!
Cook a crumby cake for me!'

> *Fairy Bow-Bells*
> I'm Fairy Bow-Bells with my tinkling song -
> Dick Whittington's special protector!
>
> I'm flying above as he trudges along,
> His permanent Bad-Luck-Corrector!
>
> I am keeping an eye on that Rotten King Rat –
> That plague-ridden flea-bag infector!
> I'm helped in my task by Miss Tiddles, the Cat,
> An astonishing rodent detector.
>
> > With a kiss and a kiss
> > And a hug and a kiss.
> > I'm Fairy Bow-bells,
> > Yes I am!

King Rat

I'm Rotten King Rat with my ear-splitting howl;
A garbage and dustbin inspector!
If I could get hold of that Fairy Bow-Bells,
To Hades I'd swiftly direct 'er!

Dick Whittington's in for a nasty surprise
In his role as a golden-prospector!
And as for the Cat, I shall never give up
Till I've ruffled and muffled and wrecked 'er!

With a hiss and a hiss,
And a howl and a hiss!
I'm Rotten King Rat,
Yes, I am!

The Emperor of Sirocco

There are hundreds of mice in the sugar 'n spice,
Dozens of rats in the stew!
They're guzzling gateaux and strawberry ice,
The meat and the vegetables too!
They crunch on the nuts and the succulent cuts,
They champ and they chomp and they chew!
They fillet the fish from the Emperor's dish,
The plundering, pilfering crew!
They descend in a hoard on our bed and our board
With an ear-splitting hullabaloo!
We're hungry and vexed and we're sorely perplexed
And we simply don't know what to do!

Rats! Rats! Mice and Rats!
We've got hundreds and hundreds
And thousands and thousands
And millions and billions and trillions and zillions of rats!
And we simply don't know what to do!

MINI-MUSICALS

Written for the children of Fox School

from **THE MIRACLE MASQUE**
Published in 1978

Mediaeval Italy: A band of war-orphans sing for their supper from town to town. In the rich city of Casteldoro they are caught up in the conflict between the wealthy towns-people and the fiery, reformist priest, Fr Renuncio.

Archangels
I saw the planets wheel about the sun;
A thousand, thousand centuries they danced and spun.
Gloria in excelsis evermore be sung –
So sayeth Gabriel on His right hand
Who is the first and last and only one.

    I saw in space the meteors flare and fade;
    A thousand, thousand centuries they glared and sped.
    Gloria in excelsis evermore be said –
    So sayeth Mic-ka-el on His left hand
    Who is the first and last whom none hath made.

I saw the blackness of infinity;
A thousand, thousand centuries like Purgatory.
Gloria in excelsis ever shall he be –
So sayeth Raphael upon His head
Who is the first and last eternally.

    I saw the human-folk upon the earth;
    Ten thousand centuries of moil and mirth.
    Gloria in excelsis – praise we all his worth!
    So sayeth Azrael upon His feet
    Who is the first and last to save us by his birth,

Children
Spring, spring, sweetest season spring.
Bird-song spring, flower-bloom spring, leaf-green spring,
Spring, spring, sweetest season spring.

Summer, summer, fairest season, summer.
Sun-blue summer, honey summer, rose-red summer,
Summer, summer, fairest season, summer.

Autumn, autumn, weeping season.
Wood-smoke, day-dusk, mist-cool autumn,
Weeping season, autumn.

Winter, winter, cruellest season, winter.
Heart-chill winter, bone-freeze winter, death-cold winter,
Winter, winter, cruellest season, winter.

Spring, spring, sweetest season spring.
Bird-song spring, flower-bloom spring, leaf-green spring,
Spring, spring, sweetest season spring.

Townspeople
Stone hearts and golden hands and jewelled eyes,
Gaze blank and blind
On want and misery.
No warmth, no love,
No pity moves or melts
Stone hearts and golden hands and jewelled eyes;
Polished as glass,
Brittle as splintered ice,
So grip, so grasp,
So clasp their riches close;
Stone hearts and golden hands and jewelled eyes;
Buried in vaults,
Prisoned in treasuries;

No sun, no star,
No ray of light to warm
Stone hearts and golden hands and jewelled, jewelled eyes.

Fr Renuncio
People of the City of Gold / Why do you search and strive
To build an earthly heaven / While still you are alive?
Dreaming of worldly paradise / Souls bear a heavy price.
Trifles and vanities cast into the flame
And purge the gold from Casteldoro's name!

People of the City of Gold / Why do you fret and scheme
To frame a hollow universe / Out of a gilded dream?
Yearning for greedy Mammon's dole / Hearts bear a heavy toll.
All wealth is trash / As light as ash.
Trifles and vanities cast into the flame
And purge the gold from Casteldoro's name!

Townspeople
Fire for the vanities / Burn all! / Shatter our gilded mirrors!
Tatter our silken robes!
The flames shall take them all! / Fire for the vanities! / Purge all!

from **THE RUSSIAN ENCHANTERS, a folk-tale**

Written with music by Rosalind Roland, 1971

Baba-Yaga, a Tartar Prince and Giant Frost pursue two children through birch forests intent on stealing the children's treasure - the secret of the New Year.

TURN! Old Year ending, ending,
TURN! Seasons ever rolling,
TURN! New Year ever coming,
TURN! TURN! TURN!

See the Old Year drag his steps,
Slowly, slowly through the snow;
Marks the snow with bitter drops,
Bent his back with dole and woe.

Giant Frost has cast his spells,
None from Winter's chains are free.
Silent is the toll of bells,
Freeze the bird, the nest, the tree.

Now the little New-born one,
Singing sweetly, singing clear –
January's Christ Child's come!
Gives us all a blithe New Year.

TURN! Old Year ending, ending,
TURN! Seasons ever rolling,
TURN! New Year ever coming,
TURN! TURN! TURN!

Baba Yaga
THUMP! THUMP! THUMP! THUMP!
Listen little children listen,
Hear a sound to freeze your mind!
Baba Yaga follows close
And sweeps away her tracks behind!
Hear the pestle, see the mortar.
Screeching winds that follow after
Speed their mistress, Baba Yaga –
Baba Yaga's close behind!
Run, little children,
RUN! RUN! RUN!

But the Baba Yaga was led astray,
And the Moujik of Twilight hid the children...

from **THE BARNSTORMERS**
Published in 1975

Winter 1840: Mr and Mrs Barnstormer and their theatrical family troupe tour Midland villages, playing in barns and halls. Their energy may be low but their spirits are high.

Strong Man's Medicine –

The Great Vesuvio
A lion bold am I,
Behold my mighty frame!
Across the vest upon my chest
You may descry my name!
My biceps bulge, but don't divulge
The secret of my Herculean Fame!

A man of steel am I,
Who bends these iron bars!
With might and main I spurn this chain
As if 'twere made of grass!
This massive length,
This giant's strength
Proclaims me as a veritable Mars!

Oh, once I was puny and lifeless,
An object of laughter and scorn.
I was scrawny and meek,
A long skinny streak,
As weak as the day I was born.
But now I've discovered the secret,
And the days of my gauntness have gorn.
I'm no longer a freak
And my elbows don't squeak…
Thanks to BIFFO, the Builder of Brawn!

'Orrible Little Blue Eyes

Angelica
My name is…
Little Lottie Leicester, with the big blue eyes,
And my chief preoccupation is with telling lies.
I just can't seem to stop it, though my loved-ones all say "drop it!"
I'm a story-telling moppet with my big, blue eyes –
With my big – blue – eyes!

I say that…
Uncle Jake's a burglar, but it isn't true.
That Mother's wheezy Pekinese was rendered down to glue!
I'm a proper little fibber, and they sure don't come much glibber
Than this talented ad-libber with my eyes of blue –
With my eyes – of – blue!

I say that…
Papa's a financier, and a rich one too!
And that Mother's maiden name was Lady Fortescue.
Though I know I'll get in trouble, get in triple, treble trouble,
Yet I can't resist a bubble while I flutter at the double
With my great big eyes of blue –
With my great – big – eyes – of – blue………………!

Tight-Rope Walkers

Nicolo & Nicolette
High wire…High wire…
Poised like a bird.
Spot-lit… High flier…
Over the void.
Stately… Step-dance…
High in the air.
Perfect… Balance…
Sky-walking there.

High Wire… High Wire…
Footsteps in space.
Higher and… Higher…
Picture of grace.
Dainty… Tip-toe…
Moths in the air.
Frozen… Statue…
Balancing there.

Crowd Watching

The company
Aaaah… Ooooh….Aaaah… Ooooh…
Look at their daring!
Look at us staring!
Setting our teeth on edge!
How can we bear it?
Look at us here
All ready to sign the pledge!

Biting our nails!
Clutching the rails!
All of us gasp out loud!
Up on our feet!
Scared us a treat!
By golly, you done – us – proud!

PARDON OUR RUBBISH
Published in 1979

Rubbish is up in arms! All things lost, discarded and trashed rise from their dumps and join with their collectors to demand greater respect. New is good but recycled is better!

Waste Merchants
We are the scrap-metal merchants!
      We are the buyers of rags!
We are the waste-paper dealers!
      The sellers of fragments and tags!
We'll borrow, beg or pinch or snitch,
Whether you're poor or filthy rich,
It doesn't matter which is which,
We're out to filch your every stitch!

In winter, summer, spring or fall,
We promise that you'll have a ball,
So pin your ears back one and all,
Here comes the old, familiar call...

      Is it old?
      Is it useless?
      Is it tattered?
      Is it torn?
      Is it dull?
      Is it boring?
      Is it ugly?
      Is it worn?

Have you wanted to sell it since the day that you were born?
Get in touch – don't delay!
Call us in right away!
We're the dealers,
The collectors.
We're the wheelers,
The connectors.
We're the jolly jazz-'n'-jumble jokers of today!

Umbrellas
Um-ber-ellas...
Um-ber-ellas...
Cinderellas...
Um-ber-ellas...
How can you lose us under your chairs?
Top deck of buses, left on the stairs,
We get the feeling nobody cares for –

Um-ber-ellas...

Newspapers
Yesterday's news –
We're just yesterday's news,
Dead as a rotten tomato.
We're found under carpets,
On newly-washed floors
And wrapping the spuds in the market...

Yesterday's news –
Is just second-hand views
Dead as a half-baked potato.
All we're fit for today is
Just chucking away,
The fate of all yesterday's dailies...

Yesterday's news –
Full of old interviews,
Written by those who are paid to.
We're slung into cupboards
And wardrobes and shelves:
The treasure of Old Mother Hubbards........

Junk Jewels
We're - the - jingles and jangles,
The sparkles and spangles
That give such a fillip
To the darkest of days!
      We glow and we flicker,
      We flash and we glitter,
      We're brash and we're tawdry
      And dazzle your gaze.
We're cheap and we're brassy,
We're shiny and glassy,
Bedizening with our displays!

We're - the - swanks and the swaggers,
The struts and the staggers
That give such a gusto
To the days and the nights!
We're nice and we're jaunty,
We're naughty and flaunty,
We prink and we blazon
Like a million lights!

We shimmer and twinkle,
We clash and we tinkle,
Be-dazing you with our
Delights!

So don't chuck away your jewellery,
Remember your tat is bright and new to me.
Your glass and paste
Is just my taste —
Never waste your gew-gaws, earrings, tie-pins,
Bracelets, chokers, bangles, hat-pins
Pendants, baubles, brooches, hair-pins:
Gimme, gimme, gimme, gimme,
JEWELS! JEWELS! JEWELS!.......................

LEGENDS

GALLANT SIR BEVIS *of* SOUTHAMPTON
Commissioned by Jill Meagre for the Hillside Singers, 1977

A version of the popular historical romance of the early 13th Century in story and verse which travelled from Britain through France, Spain and Italy as far as Russia and the East.

This is the tale of Bevis
In song and story told
A gallant son of Hampton
Undaunted true and bold

This is the tale of Bevis
Romance of fickle Fate
Legend of Wight and Hampton
Reckless of love or hate

They tell of a Princess of Scots / Forced by her King-father to marry
Sir Guy of Hampton / Though she loved another
Mordure Prince of Almain

In the courtship she felt only anger
In the marriage she felt only fury
In the birth of her child she felt loathing
That he was not son of Mordure

Bevis was that child / And his mother's monstrous rage / Ran through his infant veins / Like fiery ichor / Giving him superhuman strength

Hushaby Bevis
You baby like Hercules
Hushaby Bevis
Nor squander your tears
Father nor mother spares thought for your heartsease
So hushaby Bevis
Sleep banish your fears

"Hushaby Bevis
You child of my bitterness
Fount of my sorrow
And bane of my life
Would that your father were coffined and hell-bound
So that another could take me to wife!"

Hushaby Bevis
Your mother is plotting
Cunning as vixen
And subtle as snake
"Husband beware – for your death is upon you
I and my lover shall dance at your wake!"
Then Sir Guy's red-haired wife / Baked him a wicked dish of
serpent's tongues and toadstools / All sauced and garnished with
poisonous herbs / And she served it to him with a smile of murder
When he came in famished from the hunt / And after he had eaten
the last morsel / He died!

Hushaby Bevis
Ah – what shall become of you
Hushaby Bevis
And quiet your tears
Look at your mother exultant and laughing
Now there will never be end to your fears.

"Take him and slay him and feed him to vermin
Scatter his bones on the land or the sea
Do what you will with this child of my rancour
Away with him
For he is hateful to me!"

So they took Bevis away / But had not the heart to kill him / And gave
him to a childless shepherd / Who raised him – a hale and sonsy boy

Bevis boy Bevis
Thou stout and bonny mite
Why like a child
Are you not mild
Why must you kick and fight?

Now see Bevis
Ten years old
With stripling girth and temper bold
From sappy spring
To autumn gold
Bevis toils in woolly fold
        Baa Baa Baa

Frolicking lambs go free from fear
Greedy covetous neighbours groan
They learn from many a powerful clout
To leave the boy and his flocks alone
        Baa Baa Baa

Then one fateful day / Bevis hears of his mother's evil deed / And of her coming marriage to the fell Mordure / Her lover

His heart's blood boils at his father's fate
He runs swift and straight for Southampton Gate
BOOM BAM battering-ram
The child of her vengeance is seeking his dam!
Hammering rouses the keeper slow
Who opens and bids the boy to go
But devil nor angel bars Bevis – so
A mighty wallop lays the keeper low

Halloo halloo for Bevis -
Through Hampton's narrow lanes
The people chase
The children race
To catch him up again

Halloo halloo for Bevis -
He gains the castle stair
While fat and thin
Dodge out and in
A'coursing of the hare

Halloo halloo for Bevis -
That bold bad daring boy
Strides hot-head tall
Into the Hall
Alight with murderous joy

He sees his mother / Dressed in wedding white / Murmuring sweet endearments in foul Mordure's ear / Till she looks up / Sees Bevis and turns ashen-white with fear

SMASH CRASH splinter and slam
The child of her vengeance is seeking his dam!
BOOM BAM battering-ram
"Look to me mother! FOR – HERE – I – AM!"
The shepherd's staff
Winnows like chaff
Chairs tables all
Within the Hall
But men of might
Oer'whelm him quite
And soon he's bound
Upon the ground

No mercy does she show / No touch of mother love
But hustles him to Southampton water / Sells him to a Saracen
pirate-master

In chains on a slaver's ship
Sold by a hateful mother
Revenge burns like the whip
That falls upon his shoulder

"Farewell to Southampton to Calshot and Lee
Farewell to the Solent to Spithead and Wight
For my mother has sold me to dogs of the sea
And the land of my childhood is lost to my sight

"Oh it's Channel and Biscay and combers and spray
It's the salt in your hair and the reef in the bay
It is bread like a stone and a morsel of meat
Makes my heart ache for land and ground under my feet

"Oh it's Frankish and Gaelic and Almain and all
And the tongue-twisting language of far Senegal
It's the bite of the shark and the bite of the whip
When you're six years a'roving aboard of this ship"

Bevis grows to giant-size
Red of hair and blue of eyes
Arms like saplings legs like oak
Blood of fire and breath of smoke

He is prized beyond pearls for his valour and might / And at sixteen years old / The pirates present him as a gift to the Saracen Emperor of Spain – King Ermyn / Where he sits at his ease in the Alhambra palace with his beloved daughter / Josyan

Josyan – princess
Sits in beauty
Screened by marble
Fret with lilies

Josyan – princess
Pale as moonlight
By the fountain
Plucks kithara

Josyan – princess
Pale in beauty
Plucks kithara
Sighs for Bevis

Then Bevis' heart is caught / Though all must come to naught

King Ermyn frowns and smiles and frowns
On the Christian youth from the pirate ship
Questions Bevis to learn his story
Then offers in marriage his daughter's hand

But Bevis will not change his faith
Though Josyan's charms his heart beguiles
For Christendom his heart is strong
Despite King Ermyn's frowns and smiles
"Fair youth I knew your father's quality
A valiant knight of true civility
If you can prosper in the task I set
You'll get my Josyan in marriage yet

You must rid my land of the Monster-Boar of Baza"

Josyan – princess
Pale as moonlight
Weeps in anguish
Pleads for Bevis

But Bevis' spirit's high / His heart is light / So Josyan dries her tears
And arms him for the fight

"Take my gifts and take my heart
To aid you in your hard travails
A noble steed which never tires
A singing sword which never fails"

Bevis' spirit's high
His heart is light
Gallops to Baza
Hungry for the fight
With steed like Arundel
Sword like Morglay
Nought can betide but good
Upon this day

The Monster-Boar of Baza / Hears hoof-beats drumming of Bevis'
coming / Then shakes its spiky fell / Whetting its tusks, it paws the
earth and lumbers from its den / Bursts from the thicket ready for
the fray / Earth quakes with horrid squealing at the break of day

All day like battling Titans mad with blood
With reeking wounds – with grunts and wild halloo
Their struggle lasts
Then Bevis makes an end
And singing Morglay runs the monster through

Bevis young Bevis
Now grown to man's estate
You taste the sweets
Of foes' defeats
Reckless of love or hate

Then Bevis weary of his hurts lay down and slept / And in his
battle-slumber treacherous knights approached / And bound him up
like Samson fast and sure / Thinking to claim his prizes from the
King / Morglay Arundel Josyan – all three – and tell King Ermyn
that *they* slew the boar

Bevis poor Bevis
Cruel fate has brought you low
With bitter pains
Of prison chains
What is your fortune now?

Courage brave Bevis
Though three years are passing
Courage Brave Bevis
And suffer your doom
Chains will grow rusty
And dungeons will crumble
Fortune will free you
At last from your tomb

In those years Bevis' strength waxed until he was an Atlas
Then he snapped his chains and burst his prison

Halloo halloo for Bevis
His heart is full of spites
And vengeance sweet
Has sped his feet
To find the coward knights

He has reached Granada / He has gained the Alhambra / But death-
and-destruction what is this? / A wedding ceremony?

See how the bride stands drooping
Pale as a lily bloom
See how – with rude bravado
Stands forth the haughty groom

Halloo halloo for Bevis
He bellows through the crowd
"Stand up and fight
Perfidious knight
Your slaughter have I vowed!"

See how the groom grows white with terror
See how the bride has blushed with joy
See how the groom has fled forever
Leaving them love without alloy

And Josyan is his again / And Arundel is his again / And Morglay is
his again / And King Ermyn has dubbed him knight

Bevis Sir Bevis
Your quest is o'er and done
Your tender bride is by your side
Your honours all are won

And the wedding sweetmeats tasted of mint and honey / And the
fountains were scented with rose-petals / And the fretted lilies of the
marble screens / Threw shards of moonlight on the married pair

Now back they speed to England / For Bevis longs for home and the settling of scores

Gallop Sir Bevis
Your bride is beside you
Gallop Sir Bevis
Your fortunes await
Mother and lover who once dispossessed you
Now at your hands
Must meet with their fate

When they reach the English Channel / Up runs a great Goliath of a giant / Bevis draws his sword but the giant falls to his knees / And begs Bevis to take him as squire which Bevis heartily agrees to do And the Bishop of Paris christens the giant Ascupart

Ascupart Ascupart
Tread of thunder
Grim and swart
Mountain body
Tender heart
Ascupart Ascupart

Then Ascupart picks up the horses with Bevis and Josyan / And carries them over the water on his shoulders / So they come to Southampton / And for all his strength Bevis wept

Again I see Hampton and Calshot and Lee
Again I see Solent and Spithead and Wight
After many a year I've returned from the sea
And the land of my childhood's at last in my sight

And when they came to the castle / Ascupart breathed upon the great oaken doors / And they fell down flat! / Then Bevis began his last hunt of revenge against his mother and Mordure of Almain

"Come out come out fell Mordure
The charnel-house awaits!
Where'ere you hide
You will be spied
By swift and cruel fates!
I hear you weep
I see you creep
And fall upon your knees
'Oh, grant me life and spare my wife'
You beg with piteous pleas
Come out come out fell Mordure
Morglay is singing strong
And needs must sup
From your life's cup
To right my father's wrong!"

When Bevis' mother saw Mordure slain she fled to the tower of the
castle / But as Bevis reached her she leapt from the battlements to
certain death

Her red locks float
Like a flaming brand
Upon the wintry air
Like a burial-wreath
On the rocks beneath
Lie the strands of her scarlet hair
And she is gone forever
Who flung her life away
'Who dices with the devil
At last is made to pay'

This is the tale of Bevis
In song and story told
A gallant son of Hampton
Undaunted true and bold

This is the tale of Bevis
Romance of fickle Fate
Legend of Wight and Hampton
Reckless of love or hate.

from **THE BLACKSMITH AND THE CHANGELING**

Commissioned in 1977 by David Johnston

The magic-haunted borders of Scotland. A blacksmith returns home to find his beloved son stolen by faeries and a whining, twisted changeling in his place.

The Blacksmith's Incantation-Chant

Wayland, give me power and strength of arm
To save my son before he comes to harm!
With bible, dirk and rowan branch
To Burgh Hill I'll foot it;
Carry the cockerel, dead asleep,
And in the doorway put it.

Now cold steel in the greensward
To keep the door ajar!
The cockerel on the threshold
To wake the morning star
In I creep, stairway steep
With my eye to pry and peep.

Hark to the music, sweet, sweet music
Hark to the music that's stolen my son,
There he stands magic bound,
Trapped by the trilling that never is done.

Heel and toe,
Heel and toe,
See the elfin dancers swinging;

Light as sparks,
To and fro
To the hammer gaily ringing.
Fiddle play

Reel away
Hark to faerie voices singing.

Heedless night
Heedless day
See the grass green slippers springing
Toe and heel,
Toe and heel,
Dancing that will last forever
Light as sparks,
Elfin reel,
Music that is silent never.

Dulcet chime
Beating time
Syrup sweet is dancing fever
See them spin
Out and in
In the dance that lasts forever
Toe and heel,
Toe and heel,
See them dancing toe and heel

(the cockerel crows three times)

Yet your door is open wide
The imps of night have fled and flown
And heav'ns bright angels wait to come inside.
Ha, ha! You cannot close the door
The cold steel holds it still
So give me back my son again
And you shall have your will!

My son, my son!
So do I claim my own!
Speak to your father lad – but one word!
This human voice cannot be heard!
Their spell's upon him still – dumb and stark...

BURD ELLEN AND CHILDE ROLAND
Written for 3's Company Plus, 1976

A reworking of the old Northumbrian/Scottish folk-tale.

Northland windbound
Borderland Elfbound

Last year
Past year
Rolls the tale from tongue to ear
Spinning wheel
Running reel
Winds the dance
Upon the heel

Three King's sons
    Each one doughtier than the last
Ellen their cherished sister
By no other maid surpassed
Rufus and Ralph
The first and second be
Then Roland comes
Dubbed Childe
Yet boldest of the three

Burd Ellen
Sweetest face and lightest foot
Burd Ellen
From Bamburgh Keep to Alnwick moat

Light on the grass blade
Dancing dancing
Pearl on the dewdrop
Clinging glancing
Clover honey
Sweet as kissing
Heart's light
Heart's love
All the world loves Ellen

      She plays in the churchyard
      Caught by the Elfwind
      Chases her shadow
      Her spring evening shadow
      Caught by the Elfwind

Hawk on the high cloud
Watching
Watching
Lark in the meadow
Rising
Singing
Sees no danger
Heeds no warning
Dark might
Dark love
Elfland's Lord loves Ellen

Then she runs widdershins
      Widdershins
Widdershins
      All about the church
Caught by the Elfwind

Feels the Elfking's breath upon her
Faery darkness falls upon her
Is spun away through night and day
From Middle Earth is reft away
In Elfland's darkling Tower
To stop and stay

The cheerful flame is dead
      The hearth is bare
And bitter teardrops
      Fall upon the ashes of despair

Where is Burd Ellen
Oh where is our lark?
Lost to the Middle Earth
Lost in the dark
Who will go seek for her?
Who search her out?
Father and mother
Shall weep for her
Weep for her
Lost in the dark

We'll bring Burd Ellen back
Find her we will
First son and second son
Speed to the Hill
Straight are they magic-tied
Spellbound and still
Mother and father
Shall weep for them
Weep for them
Lost in the Hill

The wise one speaks in Roland's ear
       Your father's sword called Never-Struck-in-Vain
Take to the churchyard at the hour
    When day and night are met
Go widdershins widdershins
      And you will find
Your feet upon the path to Elfland set

Who'ere you meet
Whatever shape
The truth must speak
And honest answer make
      So ask the way of every elf you see
Their answer done
    Draw sword
And make an end
    Of each and every one

Up leaps Roland – youngest son
Father your broadsword give me
Mother your blessing shrive me
I'll bring them back to you
Find them I will
All of your children I'll bring to you
Safe to you
Back from the Hill

The fire-red nugget of the sun
      Slips from the sunset's forge into the dark
Is half consumed
      And now day's knell is rung
While Roland
Fretting – waits upon his mark

Then – soft as sin the Elfwind stirs his locks
And he runs widdershins widdershins
All about the church...

Is spun away through twilight's shadowy net
Until he finds his feet upon the path to Elfland set

A glowering land where no birds fly
Where rampant brambles bar the way
Where tangled thorn trees blot the sky
Where is no night nor yet no day
To cheer the traveller passing by

On go
On go
Childe Roland must go
Not slow
Not slow
But measuring his pace

Out pops a head from the yew tree spread

Here I be
Here I be
The Elfking's cattleherd you see

Hail to you bright elf
    Tell me in truth
In truth of Christian humankind
    Which onetime asked
Must every elfling bind
    Along which path by briar or brush confined
The Elfking's Tower of Darkness will I find?

That way
That way
The green mound's not far away

Here's your reward from Never-Struck-in-Vain!

Snick snack - through and through
Blessed blade of metal true
Slice this goblin quite in two
Away with you - away with you!

Found out
Found out
Widdershins and roundabout
Smote me with a Christian word
Slew me with a Christian sword

On go
On go
Childe Roland must go
Not slow
Not slow
But measuring his pace

Now Never-Struck-in-Vain
Has laid them low
To right and left
By might and main
Then
Before Roland's face
In the faery place
There rises up
Smooth as glass
Green as grass
The Elfin mound

With the Dark Tower atop
And a bright faery horn
Before it on the ground

The wise one speaks in Roland's inner ear
Take up the horn
Whose note was never heard
By Christian breath alone
Its music may be stirred

Speaks the horn as sweet as pain
    Grows and dies and fades again
In broken shadows on the faery plain

Within the hillock
Straight he sees a stair
And boldly enters
Eager for his prize
From room to jewelled room
He searches there
Till on the great hall's threshold stops he in amaze

    Statues three does he see
    The first is Rufus' likeness
    Next is Ralph's
    Last
    Fairest one
    Burd Ellen's image-self

    Only the eyes within the faces move
    Begging in silent anguish
    For deliverance from the Elf

FEE FI FOH FUM

Thunderous tread from Hell the Tower shakes

FEE FI FOH FUM

Deadening terror in the blood awakes

FEE FI FOH FUM
I smell the blood of a Christian
Be he asleep or be he wake
His bone-meal shall my bannock make

Then gathers Roland in his hands
The cross-carved hilt of Never-Struck-in-Vain
And so begins the contest be'twixt these two
The Elfking and the prince of Middle Earth

The thunder of their conflict
Shakes the Hill
And showers of steel-struck sparks
    Like falling rain
Illumine all the shadowy hall around
    Lighting the captives of the Middle Earth

But Roland's sun has risen in the sky
And Elfland's comet plunges to the death

Then calls the Elfking in his sundering voice

DEMONS AND DEVILS
Click clack

KOBOLDS AND URCHINS AND FIENDS

BOGIES AND BROWNIES
Click clack

COME TO MY AID
ALL YOU WEIRD AND UNCANNY
YOU SPECTRAL UNEARTHLY
DEMONIAC KINSMEN AND FRIENDS

Out of the air
Do they appear
Sharp tooth
Pricked ear
Agleem with wicked eyes
    Hang like a shroud
    A squeaking cloud
Till Roland cries

Go back your ways to Hell
Puny perfidious ants
Back to your holes
Away
Begone
Avaunt
My work is with your master
GO

Traces a triple cross with his sword's point
And lo
They're gone
Elfland is fallen and all its power is done
So lies my blade on your life's thread
    Give me my sister and my brothers back
    Free them in truth from every spell and charm
    Or by this sword which never struck in vain

You're dead!

Upon these words the Elfking gives him best
In hoarse and painful words this rune expressed

Hair of head
Nor hair of hide
Nor tear shed
Nor tear dried
Nor aught of humankind beside
Shall cleave your kinsmen to my side

The sleepers wake
And shrug to aching life
Till Roland – urgent
Speeds them from the hall

So fly they to the Tower's outer door
    There Roland turns
And drives the blade of Never-Struck-in-Vain
    Up to its cross-hilt in the threshold floor
Leaving the Elfking pent within the Tower
A prisoner of the Hill for evermore

Rufus and Ralph
Burd Ellen
They are spun away
Through night and day
In Middle Earth
To stop and stay

Their feet scarce touch the ground for joy of home
But Roland lags
    Looks back the way he's come

The wise-one's words are buzzing in his mind until his head is
ringing with the sound

Never forget… forget… forget… your father's blessed sword
Upon the Elfking's threshold have you set

The wine is supped
The fire is cold
The dance is done
The story's told

from **CIRCE BEGUILED**
Commissioned by Christopher Keyte, 1978

In the pine woods outside Circe's Palace, towards evening, Odysseus thinks himself alone, but Circe is his mocking shadow.

Odysseus:
Nestor! Atreus!
Our ship awaits us
Empty below the shore
The great adventure calls us
We must stay no more!

Comrades the feasting is over!
Has her red wine enchanted your brain?
Does her gold and her glamour still hold you?
Does the spell of her music remain?
Are you beasts, that you wallow in thraldom
While our destiny draws you again?
Never say you've forgotten our questing
How long must I call you in vain?

Circe! Witch woman!
Where are my friends?

Circe:
Your friends?

Odysseus:
No smooth words. No dissembling.
Only truth!

Circe:
For truth!
You only wish for truth?

Why then, forsooth
You truly shall have truth!
Look, look at your friends!
Transformed to beasts uncouth.
Their souls stripped bare
With snout or claw or tooth,
With bristled rump or hoof or matted hair
These are your noble friends in very truth!

Odysseus:
She twists her blade of truth within my heart.

Circe:
What is this I feel? This pain, this smart
As if truth's dagger point had pricked my heart.
Call them, Odysseus, call them each by name.
They have no stomach now for hazard's game

They swill and gorge themselves on food and wine,
Lolling, luxurious, like so many swine;
In piggish chorus snore with grunts and sighs
And never dream to quit their gilded styes!

Odysseus:
She Devil,
Evil incarnate

Circe:
See what a crew you have
How fair and strong;
And will they serve you well,
This squealing throng?
And with their trotters will they ply their oars?
And man the rigging with their furry paws?

Odysseus:
Now will I kill her!

Now blot out her sweet seductive
Voice that draws the strength of will
From out the soul of every human man that hears her sing,
Now will I kill sweet Circe!

Circe:
Odysseus, No!

Odysseus:
I have thrown off your lure.
Circe, choose death or life.
My resolution's sure
My comrades are the price!
Now break your necromancer's wand
And with it sever every magic bond.

Circe:
There, it is done
All Circe's power is for ever gone
Yet stay, Odysseus, stay for one little day?

Odysseus:
All Circe's power is for ever gone
I shall not weep until tomorrow's morn!
Nestor! Atreus! Polites!
All is well? All is well?
Let us set sail before the light is fled.

Circe:
And with the sunset Circe's heart lies dead.

Odysseus:
Nestor, Atreus
Our ship awaits us.
Empty below the shore
We must stay no more.

ENTERTAINMENTS

for Elizabeth Connell

St GEORGE AND THE DRAGON
Commissioned 1978

Maiden, fair maiden,
A' wand'ring and weeping;
Tell me, ah tell me
How came you to be
Alone by the lakeside
Alone and despairing?
I long to discover your sad history.

(Red is the cross as the blood of the martyrs,
White is the ground as the salt of the sea.
Far were the lands of your birth and your dying
Your life and your sainthood, your mystery.)

Oh sir, I beseech you
Beware the dread dragon!
I beg you to leave me,
Alone to my death.
For I have been chosen to die for my city:
Be torn by its teeth
And be burned by its breath.

Fear not my lady
Your virtue has saved you
From tearing of talons,
From fury of flame.
The sword of my Saviour will slay the dread dragon
When your kith and your kin
Are baptised in Christ's name.

(Red is the cross as the blood of the martyrs,
White is the ground as the salt of the sea.
Far were the lands of your birth and your dying
Your life and your sainthood, your mystery.)

Brave knight and champion
Obey will I gladly
And do as you bid me
Though shrinking with awe.
I'll leash the dread dragon
With my slender girdle
Nor faint at the sight
Of its sulphurous maw.

Now die, wicked wyvern
Now die on my spear-point,
So quench I forever the scourge of your flame.
The souls of this city
Are promised salvation
St George rides to rescue
In Christendom's name!

(Red is the cross as the blood of the martyrs,
White is the ground as the salt of the sea.
Far were the lands of your birth and your dying
Your life and your sainthood, your mystery.)

for **THE WORSHIPFUL COMPANY** *of* **BARBERS**
Commissioned 2010

As I was coming here today
I heard my Guardian Angel say
'A safer place you could not be
Than in the Barbers' Com-pan-ee.
If you should fall and break an arm
Or throw a fit, or come to harm,
Break out with hives or chicken-pox –
The place is chock-a-block with docs!
No matter what the medical emergency,
They're bound to treat you with the utmost urgency!'

There's a heav'nly Barber Shop –
In the sky...
Where angelic barbers strop –
As they fly...
And they harmonise each hymn
As they shave the Cherubim...
It's the first thing that you hear
When you die... Oh me. Oh myyyyy.

And do we die!...operatically speaking...sopranos mostly (and
sometimes mezzos)
So where are *you all* when we need you?

Now, Opera is littered with heroines,
Who are lovely – romantic – and damned!
Their love-lives are nerve-racking dramas,
Their boy-friends are skunks to a man (except Cavaradossi & some others).
Their mental and physical fitness
Is teetering on the abyss;
They scream and they pine and they splutter –
You can tell that there's something amiss.

99

But one thing that's true of Sopranos (and sometimes mezzos) –
Though our stage life's deplorably brief –
Never mind what condition we're suff'ring,
Our breath-control beggars belief!
We're true to Bellini and Wagner
To the very last quaver they wrote;
Though Brunnhilde's roasting and Norma is toasting,
You won't find us missing a note!
(Even Antonia, who sings herself to death for Dr Miracle, doesn't
complain: she waits to fall down dead until the end of the aria)
So,
Is there a Doctor in the House (the Opera House)?
Is there a Doctor in the House?
We're awash with dying Divas with a multitude of fevers,
Oh, there's gotta be a Doctor in the House!
There's bound to be a medic near at hand (near at hand);
Bound to be a medic near at hand.
A psychiatrist would do and perhaps a nurse or two
To attend the dying Divas with their multitude of fevers,
Oh, there's gotta be a Doctor in the House!

When you're next enjoying Faust,
        Barbers dear;
'N Margeurite is sinking fast –
        Just beware.
Though we hate to make a fuss,
Spare a thought for little us –
You are in The Opera House –
        So prepare… Oh be pre-pared!

For,
Carmen is needing employment
Since the cigarette factory closed;
She ought to give up on the smoking
And wear some respectable clothes.
Violetta should go to bed early
And go to bed *strictly* alone,
And Mimi should find better lodgings –
She coughing, and chilled to the bone!

Elvira and Anna are hopeless,
They simply can't judge men at all,
While Lucrezia poisons the people
Who casually happened to call.
Oh, what can be done with us Divas?
We're mad or we're sad or we're sick;
We peak and we pine, we whinge and we whine
We're moany and groany and thick!

Oh, where's a good physician when you need one;
Where's the GP who'll come out and hold your - hand?
No medic can be found, ready masked and gloved and gowned
Oh where's a good physician when you need one.

There's going to be an Opera operation,
Madam Butterfly needs sewing up again;
Leonora needs the stomach-pump, and Tosca's just about to jump –
There's got to be…
Yes there's got to be…
Oh, there's got to be a Doctor in the Ho.......use!

FAREWELL & GOODBYE
Commissioned for her Farewell Concert, St John's Smith Square, 2010

There are dozens of ways of saying 'goodbye',
Aloha, au'voir or adieu;
With a tremulous smile and a tear in the eye
Or a silent, 'good riddance to you!'.
But now that we've come to the parting of ways
And you think that you'll see me no more –
I hope you'll remember the happy old days,
When I'm far from Britannia's shore...

Farewell to old England, to London and Kew,
Farewell to dear friends and the life that I knew
For I'm off to Australia to start life anew,
And I'm not coming back from Down Under.

So get out your hankies
And stifle your sighs,
Restraining your tears
As you wave your goodbyes - (you can start waving NOW)
Yes, I'm off to Australia for good and for all....
And I'm NOT coming back, no I'm NOT coming back
No, I'm NOT coming back from Down Under
However......................
Farewell *doesn't* mean that my career is over;
What it means is quite the opposite in fact...
When a Diva says she's going
There's no earthly way of knowing
Just how long her going's going to protract!

If you watch me you will rapidly discover
I'll be milking every opportunity…
If a Diva says she's quitting
She should not be heard admitting
Just how over-long that quitting's going to be…
Farewell Concerts – LOTS of them!

I'll – say – 'Farewell Buenos Ares,
Farewell Oslo, Rome and Paris,
Farewell Lisbon and New York,
Farewell Amsterdam and Cork
Farewell London, Farewell Perth
Farewell Lima and Fort Worth…'
Farewell Iceland and Brazil
Have you had your Farewell fill?…………

But that's in the future,
And this is today,
And I can't help but feel
As I'm going away,
Just a twinge of regret –
Should I go?
Should I stay?

On the other hand…
Farewell means I can escape the English weather,
With its bloody unpredictability.
Goodbye traffic and pollution,
I've the ultimate solution,
I am fleeing from you far across the sea!

I'll be shot of those eternal tube suspensions,
And the road-works started every single day;
Men with shovel and with digger
Making big holes even bigger
So that every journey's 'Subject to Delay'!
And...
Oz is not a million miles away
No, Oz is not a million miles away.
You can tweet me, you can twitter,
Send me endless streams of witter.
You can email, you can page me
(Which is *certain* to engage me)
You can phone me, you can type me,
You can fax me, you can skype me
You can even – if you want to – come and stay -
'Cause Oz is not a million miles away...
So...
Farewell to old England, to London and Kew,
Farewell to dear friends and the life that I knew
For I'm off to Australia to start life anew...
Will I ever... return... from Down Under...?

But maybe...
You'd like me to come back... just once in a while?
Say you'd like me to come back?
Yes, I'll keep coming back like a favourite song
A whisper – a haunting refrain;
And I promise you won't be without me for long,
No, I shan't keep you waiting in vain.
Then - just when you fear that this song was your last,
I will burst into vision once more.
So just keep on counting the days as they pass...
Till I'm back on Britannia's shore!
Unforgettable – that's what I am!
If you say 'An era's ending', I'll reply...
That Farewell – doesn't – have - to - mean GOODBYE!!

MUSICAL PLAYS

from **THE PINK PARAKEET**

Commissioned by June Keyte for Kingsmead School, published in 1983

London 1948: Tony Marino, ex-soldier, returns home to find his father's seedy night-club on the verge of collapse, and decides to re-launch it

> *Eddie & Sally*
> Pit-pat on my windowpane,
> Look, here comes the rain again,
> Sorrows that I can't restrain
> Mingle with the rain.
>
> Memories that haunt me so,
> Old regrets from long ago;
> Heartaches never seem to go
> In the falling rain…

But –
Maybe tomorrow will be better, maybe tomorrow will be fine.
Maybe the telephone will ring and you will say –
'Hi there, sweetheart. Say we'll never part,
Say that this is just the start… that tomorrow will be fine.'

> Nothing seems to turn out right,
> World seems full of pain and spite,
> All our comfort, our delight,
> Vanished out of sight.
>
> When the sunshine hides away,
> Turns each day a doleful grey,
> Listen to that whisper say,
> 'Things may not be right…

'But –
Maybe tomorrow will be better, maybe tomorrow will be fine.
Maybe tomorrow will jump up and say to us –
Come on – break out! Here's what life's about,
Show the door to gloom and doubt and tell yourself,
Tomorrow will be fine!'

Tiger Torch Song

Rita
Hey, little boy – just watch what you're at…
Who invites a tiger for a cosy little chat?
If I don't feel like going, you can't get me to scat…
So mind how you tangle with this grown-up pussy-cat!

Do you want me to purr
My special purr?
Say, 'Pretty, please',
I shan't demur.
No need to tease,
Or cause a stir…
Just come up close
And you'll hear me… Purrrrrrrr!

Are you wary because
I show my claws –
Don't my velvet paws
Win your applause?
Maybe they're used
To settle scores.
Best keep away from my
Velvet paw..aw..aw..aws…Purrrrrrrr!

Say, little boy, why don't you stay?
Now you've caught your tiger, it is time for us to play…
If you ride on a tiger, you've surely got to pay…
'Cause kitty may start growling if you try to run away!

Do you want me to smile
My tiger's smile?
Is my tiger-smile
Not quite your style?
Don't be afraid,
Just wait awhile,
Why move away
When you see me smi..i..i..ile…Purrrrrrrr!

Do you want to admire
My eyes of fire?
Are my tiger's-eyes
Your one desire?
If I should leave
Would you expire?
Just come up close
And take time to admi..i..i..ire…Purrrrrrrr!

De-da-de-da… watch what you're at.
De-da-de-da…a cosy chat?
De-da-de-da… can't make me scat
'Cause I'm a great big, full-sized, sophisticated,
Grown-up, experienced PUSSY-CAT…Purrrrrrrrrrrr!

Waiting for a whisper

Benno the nark
When you're waiting for a whisper from the other side of town –
When you're crouching in a dustbin so the cops can't track you down –
When your choppers start to chatter as you find your cover's blown –
When you're waiting for a whisper,
  of a whisper
    of a whisper
      from the other side of town.
  I see me…
    Running around
    With my ear to the ground,
    With my eye to the keyhole
    Of the Lost and Found.
    I'm in for a penny,
    I'm in for a pound,
    Just running around
    With my ear to the ground.

When you're standing in the gutter – three a.m. or thereabouts –
When your pride is in the pawnshop and your luck is up the spout –
When the cruel world describes you as a lousy layabout –
When you're standing in the gutter –
  Three a.m.
    four a.m., or
      five a.m. or thereabouts…

  I see me…
    Cutting a dash
    When I'm out on the thrash,
    With my nose in the air
    And a fistful of cash.
    Pint of black velvet

And bangers and mash,
When I'm out on a thrash
And I'm cutting a dash.

Yeah...
Out on the thrash... cutting a dash... bangers and mash...
Ooh, I could do with some of them right now!

from **CROWDS**
Commissioned by Oakham School, published in 1987

CROWDS follows the fortune of two families – the Cottles and the Wilkins – who earn their living on the streets of London between 1918 and 1939

The Crowd
We are the crowds of the city,
We're the faces in the street.
We are the crowds of the city,
Watching glory of defeat.
      We are the throng and the rabble,
      Tower of Babel –
We are the crowd.

We are the crowds of the city,
Come to see the big parade.
We are the crowds of the city,
There when history is made.
      We see you life pass before us,
      We are the chorus –
We are the crowd.

We are the crowds of the city,
Don't believe us when we cheer.
We are the crowds of the city,
When we're smouldering, take care!
      We are the mob and the mourners,
      Destiny spawns us –
We are the crowd...
      The crowd...
         The crowd.

Music Hall Song

Dotty Day
My young fella's just come 'ome
From bloomin' foreign parts,
Fit and well… and in one piece…
It really warmed our 'earts!
But joy 'as turned to sorrow,
When 'e looked for a job…
"Land fit for heroes" so they said…
But 'e's just one of the mob…

My boy wants some honest toil,
'E wants an occupation,
Guaranteed for certain sure,
For serving of 'is nation.
They promised 'im employment
When 'e got back from the war,
But they ain't got nothin' for 'im
And they're showin' 'im the door.

'Oo's got a job for 'Arry?
'Oo's got a job for 'im?
We're dyin' for to marry,
But the future's lookin' dim.
Won't someone lend an 'and 'ere,
'Ooever it may be:
For I want marry 'Arry,
And 'e wants to marry me!

After three years overseas,
You'd think 'e'd done 'is bit,
A'fightin' in those trenches,
But not a bit of it.
They say "the war is over"...
But the battle's just begun...
The fight for jobs is just as bad...
As the fightin' 'e's just done!

My boy's got a lot of grit,
'E's not afraid of labour.
'E'll work as hard as 'Ercules,
And 'arder than 'is neighbour.
'E's tougher than old army boots,
And stronger than an 'orse.
'E's cheerful as a cricket –
And reliable – o' course!

'Oo's got a job for 'Arry? (*repeat chorus*)

Away From The Crowds

Winnie, Flo and Lily
Away from the crowds I can hear what my heart is saying...
Far from the streets I can see where I'm going to...
When I'm alone there's a voice that keeps calling... calling...
Telling me, 'Listen – I'm speaking to you'.

> As the old river runs,
> Can you hear what she's saying?
> With the turn of the tide
> Comes a voice, soft and low...
> 'Remember the past times,
> But live for the future,
> Where your hopes they will ebb
> And your dreams they will flow'.

Out on the bridge I can watch the old river running...
Far from the crowds I can hear what she says to me...
Deep in the night, while the whole world is sleeping...
She murmurs these words as she flows to the sea:

> 'Oh, never give way
> To the doubts and despairing,
> No matter how sombre
> The future may grow.
> Believe in yourself
> And your friends and your loved ones,
> Though your hopes they should ebb
> And your dreams they should flow.'

When the day's work is done - and tomorrow seems cheerless...
When happiness dims and there's nowhere to go...
Cross over the bridge – hear the old river running...
And she'll teach you to trust in the ebb and the flow.

Jarrow Hunger March

Jarrow Marchers
Down from the North East,
Down from the North East,
Down from the North we've come.

Slept on the school floors,
Fed by the people,
Down to the Southern sun.

Nowt in our bellies,
Nowt in our pockets,
Nowt for the old folks at home,
But down from the North
Where hope springs eternal,
Down from the North we've come.

Jarrow lads
March side by side.
Short of bread
But full of pride
Can Stan Baldwin
Stem the tide?
Bring work back
To Tyneside?

Down from the North East,
Down from the North East,
Down from the North we've come.
Walked till our feet ached,
Walked till our boots split,
Down to the southern sun.
Nobody asked us,
Nobody wants us,
Nobody gives us a damn!
But down from the North
Where hope springs eternal,
Down from the North we've come.

from **THE NAVAL KNIGHTS OF WINDSOR**
(*or* Restless Knights)

Commissioned for St George's Choir Windsor, 1992

*The choirboys find themselves in conflict with ghosts of the Naval Knights who
once occupied their school and were evicted for their bad behaviour.*

Drunken Naval Knights
We were rolling on down
Into old Windsor Town
With a storm up ahead
And the wind coming round;   (*Hic!*)
And none that we hailed
Was more happy than we
As we rolled and we billowed,
We billowed and rolled
We ro–ho–ho–olled into old Windsor Town!

      Now, 'The King's Head' wouldn't have us,
They said we was too lit-up.
      'The Castle Inn' said likewise,
Objecting to the hiccups   (*Hic!*)
      'The Unicorn' first took us in
Then threw us out completely –
      They dumped us in the horse-trough
(But did it rather neatly).
We tried 'The Pony', 'Crown' and 'Ship'
      From whence we was ejected,
(The landlords *had* been friendly),
      Which seemed most unexpected.
Now, by this time we'd had enough
      Which made us rather leery,
So we started being men-'o-war
      And not so airy-fairy!

We had fought a grand engagement –
(We'd left 'The Ship' a'sinking)
And was rolling back to harbour
(A touch the worse for drinking)
When THE VISITORS were on us,
Out of the clear blue skies,
With their RULES & REGULATIONS
And their wicked, beady eyes!

Naval Ghosts
When the bones and souls of shipmates
Rise up in the dream to come,
And the ghosts of ships
From the ocean deeps
Sail in from the setting sun.
The wind in their phantom rigging
Will whistle a haunting air –
When the bones and souls of shipmates
Rise up –
Rise up –
To join their comrades here.

When the din of an ancient battle
Seems to howl on the storm-tossed air;
When the cannon's blast
And the splintered mast
Have you trapped in memory's snare,
When the sight of the dead and dying
Seems grievously sharp and clear -
When the bones and souls of shipmates
Rise up –
Rise up –
To join their comrades here.

Then here you will see a terrible crew
From the graveyard depths where they rise anew
Who fought their fight and were slain or slew
And who gave their lives protecting YOU...
Yes, the bones and souls of shipmates
Rise up –
Rise up –
And join their comrades here!

St Peter and St George
'St Peter, oh St Peter are you standing at the Gate?
Is the gold key in your hand and do the trumpeters await?
Have you prepared a welcome, the best you can command?
For I've brought a boarding party of the finest in the land!'

'Oh, St George, my friend, pray tell me, are there crowns upon their heads?
Are their shoulders wrapped in ermine? Sure, they must be nobly bred.
Are there rings upon their fingers, are their tresses soft as silk?
Do they live in regal splendour off the honey and the milk?'

'Oh, St Peter, oh, St Peter, throw your Heaven's gate open wide,
For the flower of the finest I have standing by my side.
They come not from an easy life, they are not gently born,
For they lived upon the high seas, each bitter night and morn.'

Then back the heavenly gates were flung, the Poor Knights ushered in,
While choristers and cabin-boys they raised a glorious din.
The planets all went spinning in a dance beyond compare...
And paradise is richer now the Naval Knights are there!

from **THE MOST WANTED FACES**

Commissioned by June Keyte for Kingsmead School, published in 1978

1922: the New York underworld. Two incompetent gangs spar with each other while their leaders mourn their broken love-affair.

Hi-Hat gals

Ruby
Get a load of us –
Hand-me-down dames,
With second-class names
And pawnbroker diamonds and foxes…

Tootsie
This circlet of pearls,
That coils in my curls,
Once shimmered in Ruby de Rox's…

Dusty
The jewels that wink
On my rabbit dyed mink
Weren't wrapped up in Cartier boxes…

Wanda
And the toughness that hides
Our marshmallow insides
Is just one of life's paradoxes.

All
So don't judge a cake by its icing –
The first bite can be quite surprising!
Can't you see that
We're soft-centred Susies,
We're gold-hearted floosies,
We'll never desert ya,
Or harm ya, or hurt ya…

We're dream-filled gals
Just looking for a foursome of
Life… long… paaaaals!

G-Note gang

Dum-Dum
Get a load of us –
Hand-me-down guys
From our spats to our ties –
A match for our gals and our popsies.

Limey
Our rods and our gats,
Our fedora hats
All featured in second-hand shopses.

Manhattan
The automobile
He's trying to steal
Is bound to be stopped by the copses…

Notches
And the hold-ups I planned
(Theoretically grand)
Turn out diabolical flopses.

All

So don't judge a rat by its poison…
The first bite can be quite suproisin!
Can you see
We're all soft-centred laddies,
We're gold-hearted baddies,
We'll never desert ya,
Or harm ya, or hurt ya…
We're good ol' pals…
Just looking for a foursome of
Good… time… gaaaaaals!

Venus

I'm Venus Ventura,
A high-class doll –
No glitter - no fuss – no display…
I'm Venus Ventura,
I'm no one's moll,
I play the games *I* want to play!

Long ago
I knew a guy –
Was the apple
Of my eye…
Every time
He held my hand –
Took me to Cloud-Cuckoo Land…
But that was a long, long time ago…

I can't help
Remembering –
How I had him
On a string.
Then I found
The bird had flown –
Knew that I was on my own…
Yes, that was a long, long time ago…

124

Every day that
Passes now –
Makes me think of
Him, somehow…
Makes me think about that guy –
And the day we said 'goodbye'…
But, that was a long, long time ago…

Poppa and Mama

Poco Poppa Pizza
And Mama Picollo!
Feudin' an' a' fightin'
Most any place they go!
Sometimes yelling FORTE!
And sometimes *piano*!
Poco Poppa Pizza
And Mama Picollo!

In Roma
Shazom-a!
They go down like a bomb-a!

In Napoli
Slap-happily –
They're trading insults snappily!

Milano –
Shazam-o!
They shout and stamp and slam-o!

In Sicily.
So fizzily –
Their tempers popping busily!

Poco Poppa Pizza
And Mama Picollo!
Feudin' an' a'fightin'
Most any place they go!
Sometimes yelling FORTE!
And sometimes *piano*!
Poco Poppa Pizza... and Mama Picollo!

from **MISTRESS OF CHARLECOTE**
Commissioned by Putney High School, 1996

Mary Elizabeth Lucy relives the events of her life, from young love and heartbreak to the ups and downs her years as Mistress of Charlecote

The Sunshiny Morning of Youth

Mary Elizabeth Lucy
In the sunshiny morning of youth,
When everything's right with the world,
And your heart sings with joy
For the love of a boy
It's the sunshiny morning of youth.

Oh, that first jubilation of youth,
That holiday, skylarking life -
When nothing seems sad
And everything's glad –
That's the sunshiny morning of youth.

> Then...
> When duty calls,
> That stern commander,
> When sober sense
> Must rule your heart.
> How hard it is
> To leave your lover,
> Break your vows –
> Forever part.

But when at last
You lift your spirit,
Set your mind
To do what's right;
Don't look back,
Don't glance behind you,
Vain regrets
Are bane and blight.

When the sun sets, at last, on your youth,
When the shadows creep into your heart,
Put the darkness to flight
And remember how bright...
Was the blissful
And joyous
The hopeful
And rapturous
Sunshiny morning of youth.

Dessert!

Lucy's children
There are sweetmeats and syllabubs,
Sherbets and splits.
Souffles and sauces and sponges.
And syrups so sweet
They are torture to eat
And torment you
With terminal twinges.

There are candies and chocolate,
Custards and creams;
Cheesecakes and charlottes and crumbles.
And a surfeit of cake
That will give you toothache,
While bringing on
Collicky rumbles.

There are jellies and junkets,
Trifles and tortes,
Russes and mousses and moulds.
Pancakes and puddings,
Pastries and pies,
With ices
All freezingly cold.

Then marshmallow, marzipan,
Fondants and fudge,
There are toffees and Turkish delice.
Pink sugared almonds
And peppermint creams
And caramel-coconut-ice.

There are myriads more
Of confections galore –
The fools and the flummeries,
Buns and blancmanges,
The tansies and tarts
And gingerbread hearts,
The sundaes and snows –
The dumplings and doughs –
A crystallized violet,
A pink sugar rose......

Dessert! Dessert! Dessert!

Poor Folk's Food

Estate tenants
There is one sauce that poor folks have
Will never lose its savour,
And that is Hunger, sharp as sin,
Which gives our food its flavour.

Poor folk's food,
Poor folk's food.
Hunger's the spiciest
Sauce of the lot
For poor folk's food.

Crust and scrape for breakfast,
Nothing at all for tea.
Cabbage and pots in a stew for sup,
With a bit of a bone,
An overcooked bone
A gristly bone if we're lucky.

When Mistress Lucy visits us
She brings what she is able.
Some broth, some bread, some broken meats,
The crumbs from the rich man's table.

Rich folk's food,
Rich folk's food.
Filled to the brim
And spoilt for choice
With rich – folk's – food.

Boddlewyddan

Mary Elizabeth
I remember Boddlewyddan,
River Clwyd running free;
And the air of Boddlewyddan
Is my sweetest memory.

Now my home's the heart of England,
And the land is fair to see;
But the air of Boddlewyddan
Is my sweetest memory.

Though the Midland fields are fertile
And the skies are wide and flat.
Though it's folk are kind and stolid
And the Midland cattle fat...

Under Clwyd's blue and windy
Heaven is where I long to be,
For the air of Boddlewyddan
Is my sweetest memory.

Ah, my heart still yearns for Clwyd,
For the savour of the sea
In the air of Boddlewyddan
Is my sweetest memory.

CHAMBER
OPERAS

from **LUNCH AT THE COOKED GOOSE**
Commissioned by Definitely Divas, 2000

The 25 year reunion of four women who once shared a flat as music students.
They reminisce, bicker and get drunk in a smart restaurant while waiting for
the food.

Crystal
Reunion?
What on earth was I thinking about!
Reunion –
There's no hope of this lunch working out.
Reunion –
Why on earth should they care what we eat?
It's the fault of my wretched conceit
Which refuses defeat,
I cajole and entreat
And insist that we meet
For this pointless – Reunion!

Gwyneth's Late!

Crystal, Maggie and Heather
Late for concerts,
Late for classes,
Lost her music,
Lost her glasses –
Never known to be on time if she can help it!
Misses trains
And misses buses,
Just can't see
What all the fuss is.
Never known to be on time if she can help it!

Gwyneth (offstage)
I **can't** help it!

> *Crystal, Maggie and Heather*
> Late for friends
> And late for tutors,
> Impresarios
> And suitors –
> One thing's certain
> They will have to hold the curtain,
>> For Gwyneth's never been on time,
>> Never, ever been on time,
>> Never known to be on time,
>> Never, never known to be on time...
>> If she can help it!

Gwyneth (offstage)
I **can't** help it!

Student days

Maggie
The things about college
That stick in my mind are
Being hungry, and the
Awful smell
Of the tutors' rooms...
> *Gwyneth*
> Professor Wagstaff,
> Tuna and onion sandwiches...

Heather
Melinski,
Oranges and aftershave...
> *Maggie*
> Wilson-Bede,
> Peppermints and BO...

Crystal
Mannheim,
Salami and cigars!

Maggie, Gwyneth, Heather & Crystal
After twenty-five years... (Think of twenty-five years!)
What we remember the best... (There's no way we'd forget!)
Is not our musical muse...
The operatic joke and the jest... (Repeated ad nauseam!)
After twenty-five years... (It's a hell of a long time!)
What comes back to us only too well... (You don't have to remind us!)
Isn't the scales or the songs... (Not the scales *or* the songs.)
But the *stench* – it was HELL!

A Toast!

Crystal, Gwyneth, Heather & Maggie
Let's drink a Toast to Love –
The pain, the pleasure and the loss.
A rousing Toast to love –
The pure, the carnal and the dross.
Let's drink a Toast to Men –
The grand, the gorgeous and the gross.
A Toast to Men and Love –
The boy, the partner or the boss.

Let's drink a Toast to Life –
The frantic, fast or furious.
A triple Toast to Life –
The high, the low, the glorious.
Let's drink a Toast to Life, to Men, to Love –
But most of all, to Love....................................

Gwyneth's love life

Heather
What was your wedding like, Gwyn?

Gwyneth
My *weddings*, you mean...
In Cincinnati with Chuck
The guests were running amok –

In Sydney harbour with Dale
Our nuptials ended in jail!
My Hamburg marriage to Horst
Was a disaster, of course;
Is it surprising they all ended in divorce?

After divorce number three
I tasted sweet liberty.
I swore an oath to myself
I'd live my life on the shelf.
I'd turn my heart into stone
And fight my battles alone...
Then I was ambushed by a sexy saxophone!

Baritones and basses
Buzz off! Scarper! Scram!
Tenors take a ticket!
I'm – OK – as – I – am.............

Another Toast!

Crystal, Gwyneth, Heather & Maggie
Let's drink a Toast to Lunch –
The plain, the rich, the Cordon Bleu.
A rousing Toast to Lunch –
Nouvelle Cuisine or Epicure.
      Let's drink a Toast to Wine –
      The white, the red, the fizzy stuff.
      The wine we drink at Lunch –
      The new, the vintage or the rough.
Let's drink a Toast to Friends –
The ones we love or love to hate.
A triple Toast to Friends –
The ones invariably late!
Let's drink a Toast to Life, to Friends, to Love, to Men, to Wine –
And finally a Toast to LUNCH...

from **WELCOME TO PURGATORY**
Commissioned by 3 in a Bar, 2003

In an ante-room to the Court of Purgatory, Mary Queen of Scots and Elizabeth the 1st quarrel, confide and condole with each other while waiting to learn who will go to hell.

Murderess! Traitor!

MQS	Murderess!
ER	Traitor!
M	Blasphemer!
E	Whore!
M	Bastard!
E	Adulteress!
M	Usurper!
E	Subverter of Law!
M&E	Usurper! Subverter! Usurper! Subverter of Law!
E	Light-o'-Love!
M	Cold heart!
E	Lascivious!
M	Bitch!
E	Papist!
M	Dissenter!
E	Hysteric!
M	Heretical witch!
M&E	Hysteric! Heretic! Hysteric! Heretical witch!
E	So, Cousin?
M	Yes, Cousin?
M&E	Who's word will they take?

E	A Stuart's?
M	A Tudor's?
E	Tarantula!
M	Snake!
E	So, Cousin?
M	Yes, Cousin?
E	Do you shudder and shake?
M	Doesn't Hellfire…

Giovanni Biscotto (breaking in)
There's no peace with these two at each other's throats!
It's ever like this with Princes,
They *must* be in the right.
Stiff-necked and overweening,
Blind to each other's plight.
Machiavelli, my master,
Studied them hour by hour:
Saw what they desired the most –
Power for the sake of Power!

Love in the Heart / Love in the Head

Mary
In the heart, in the heart
Always love in the heart;
The dizzying madness of love in the heart.
The vows and the promises
Never to part...
Then the fading and dying
Of love in the heart.

       Three husbands had I
       But only one friend...
       And little David Rizzio,
       Sweet David Rizzio,
       Only David Rizzio
       My broken heart could mend.

But no, no, no,
It was never meant to be
That little David Rizzio
Should ever bed me.

Elizabeth
In the head, in the head,
Always love in the head.
Oh, the rapturous visions
Of love in the head.
The wooing, pursuing
The vows left unsaid –
Then the fading and dying
Of love in the head.

No husband I had,
But one loving friend
And bonny, gallant Robin,
Sweet and gallant Robin,
Only gallant Robin
My lonely heart could mend.
But no, no, no,
It was never meant to be
That sweet and gallant Robin
Should ever wed me.

We Will Not Speak!

Giovanni Biscotto
If you both refuse to bear witness they cannot condemn you.

Elizabeth & Mary
Let them thunder
Cajole or upbraid.
Let them threaten,
Accuse or harangue.
My cousin
Will come to my aid
By steadfastly
Holding her tongue.

Let them warn of
Damnation and Hell.
Let them bully,
Arraign and enquire.
We'll be staunch in
Our silence, although
They promise us
Brimstone and fire!

We will not speak.
It is our right!
Our lips are sealed
To their despite!
We are resolved
To stop our mouths…

We will not speak!

145

from **FLOATING**
Commissioned by Divas 2, 2003

A power failure in the Floatation-suite of a Health Spa brings two contrasting personalities, Leandra and Gabby into collision as they wait for light and heat to return.

Mrs Ultra Undies

Gabby
Manager? I *own* 'Ultra Undies' of Knightsbridge, Paris and New York!

I've got bras of every kind,
Some fasten front and some behind.
I've got balconettes and half-cups,
Underwired with really vast cups.
I've got bustieres, bikinis,
Minimisers, padded 'teenies'.
I've got every brassiere you could desire –
Bras for absolutely every shape of buyer.

> I am Mrs Ultra Undies,
> (Open every day but Mondays)
> I'm a legend in the world of lingerie (*pronounced 'linjeray'*)
> My boutique's the word for 'chic'
> From Manhattan to Mustique,
> With a price tag only super-rich will pay.
> I have customers galore,
> Queues around the block and more;
> I have all and sundry asking for advice…
> But you're sure to hear me say as I turn the mob away –
> 'You can't have the goods if you can't pay the price'.

I've got corsets fit to kill
In PVC or silk or twill.
I've got waspies, stays and cinches
Guaranteed to lose you inches.
I've got baby-dolls (and teddies
Only fit for baddies beddies),
I've got peek-a-boos to help you let off steam –
Can-can petticoats that make you want to scream!

Yes, I'm Mrs Ultra Undies,
Lady-boss of sultry fundays,
I'm a legend in the world of lingerie.
My French-knickers are discreet,
They're a city-slicker's treat,
With a price tag only super-rich will pay.
Oh, my scanties and my thongs
Drag in countless panty-throngs,
I have all and sundry begging for advice,
And you're sure to hear me roar as they're pouring
through the door –
'You can have the goods, if you just pay the price'!

Turning Sceptical

Leandra
I don't have a byline, I'm simply 'Leandra' but when I first
joined FRIG Magazine I had some hard lessons to learn.

I started off enthusiastic –
It wouldn't do.

I tried hard-bitten, brash, bombastic –
Wisecracking too.

I'd be witty and earnest and gloomy and gay.
Depressed in the evening and manic next day;
Till they took me aside and attempted to say
In their clever, ironical FRIG-frosty way,
'If you're hoping for copy that's classé, my dear
You must make it a trifle more glacé – that's clear.
Elliptical hauteur is what you're aiming to achieve,
So shed that warm, endearing voice,
Try for... objective, cold as ice.
But above all else,
Leandra dear,
Be sceptical.'

Turning sceptical
   Flipped my ego upside-down
Made me dyspeptical,
   Fishy eyed and acid tongued.
Had to lose my cheery grin,
Turn my optimism in,
Joie-de-vivre was mortal sin
When turning sceptical.

So now I'm a cynic and classic'ly cool.
I'm everyone's 'dahling' but nobody's tool.
When some imprudent critic insists on a duel,
My regular readership gloatingly drool
At my deadly dispatch of the hot-headed fool,
Which is elegant, stylish – and frequently cruel.

Yes, I am sceptical,
    Never eager or extreme;
An ice receptacle –
    Tiger prawn with sour cream.
You'll never see *me* twist and shout
    Or hang more flags and bunting out...
But I *do* beg leave to doubt –
Because I'm sceptical.

Multi-therapy

Gabby and Leandra

G   Have a go at something *new*... (*dances*)
          Did you try Yoga?
L   Kept falling over...
G   Yogic flying?
L   Far too trying...
G   Meditation?
L   No concentration...
G   Regression?
L   Ooh – the depression.
          I'm telling you,
          None of them work!

G   I've done -Hydrotherapy,
          Hypnotherapy,
          Aromatherapy,
          Physiotherapy,
          Colour Analysis,
          Psychoanalysis,
          Acupuncture and all.

L   I've done Reflexology,
          Osteology,
          Gynaecology,
          Podiatology,
          Orthopraxy,
          Dermiopraxy,
          Acupuncture and all.

G&L (*dancing*)
Ai, ai, ai. Ai, ai, ai. Acupuncture and all.

L   Epsom Salts, you are my destiny,
        For all your faults, you save my sanity.
        Wrap me up in tranquillity,
        You miraculous Epsom Salts.

        Magnesium Sulphate, you are here to stay;
        Banish the blues and float the grey away.
        Purge my problems, save the day,
        You miraculous Epsom Salts.

G&L (dancing)
        Ai, ai, ai. Ai, ai, ai. Acupuncture and all. Hey, Hey!

from **A FLIGHT OF PILGRIMS**
Commissioned by Barry Collett, East Midland Opera, 1990

11.00 pm: 7 pilgrims on a Cathedral Tour, wait in the departure lounge of a small European airport for their plane to be repaired: they are all seeking consolation.

Thomas - (in a wheelchair)
At least God got us here safely.

When you consider, my friend –
When you consider the tragedy headlines:
'Airliner Falls From The Sky',
'Tidal Wave Sweeps Away Thousands'.
When you consider, my friend,
The daily catastrophes
Plunging upon us,
It would be easy to sit down and weep...
And yet –
God is good,
God is here,
With us;
God with care
Has brought us through the air,
Safely.
When you consider, my friend –
When you consider the TV disasters:
'Bushfires Threaten The City',
'Hurricane Inundates Islands'.
When you consider, my friend,
How hourly calamities
Bring devastation,

It would be easy to sit down and weep.
And yet –
God is good...
At least he got us here safely.

Mrs Mendoza (laughing)
Yes, that is something in his favour!

I met Mr Mendoza...
He was my fourth husband,
And rather old...

In Rio –
There was sadness in the air,
In Rio –
There was gladness everywhere.

When we met,
We were two abandoned hearts
In Rio...

And Christ
Watches over the city...
Arms spread wide;
Watching over the city.
His arms are enfolding the city,
In Rio...

In Rio –
There was madness in the air,
In Rio –
There was sadness and despair.
When he died
He abandoned me to life
In Rio...

In Rio –
Is there sadness in the air?
In Rio –
Is there gladness or despair?
When I left
I left more than just my heart
In Rio...

Thomas... do you remember a time
When you could walk?

Thomas
I remember...
Rolling down a grassy bank when I was very little...
Getting up... laughing
And laughing... I remember
Climbing up the bank again and again...

Mrs Mendoza
How old were you
When you had polio?

Thomas
Five years old.

Mrs Mendoza
Poor little Thomas...
Poor little boy.

Thomas
Later, I remember
Thinking of that grassy bank
And wondering if I would ever
Roll down it again –
For some reason
It seemed important
That I should.

Some children... young people,
Dream of flying... driving a car.
I used to dream of walking –
Especially climbing up that bank
And rolling down.

Mrs Mendoza
Do you still dream?

Thomas
Oh, no. Not now.
My wheelchair stopped the dream.
Imagine!
A travel courier in a wheelchair!

Faith...
Where do we find faith?
In the heart?
Or the head?
Or the board?
Or the bed?
Faith...
Where do we find faith?

Love...
Where do we find love?
In the head?
In the soul?
In the part?
Or the whole?
Love...
Where do we find love?

The Pilgrims
The sun is rising!
Day is here at last!
Day... another day.
The sun is rising,
Welcome the new day
Fresh hopes and hopes renewed,
Another day.
Look at the sun!
Look at the sky!
The sun is rising,
Day is here again!

BRUNEL

The Opera

from **BRUNEL The Opera**
Commissioned by the Janice Thompson Performance Trust, 2005

An evocation of some of the great engineer, Isambard Kingdom Brunel's achievements in bridge, railway and ship building, and the cost to him and his workers.

Isambard Kingdom Brunel
For my tunnels and bridges,
Tracks and trains,
Cutting and railway town...
Through hedges and ditches,
Banks and lanes,
Up the hills and down.
Survey, Survey! En Avent!
I must find the smoothest way
For my tunnels and bridges,
Tracks and trains,
And none shall say me nay!

For my docks and slipways,
Boats and ships,
Millwall to Bristol Town.
Financial parlays,
Business trips
Up the Severn and down.
Money, Money! En Avent!
I must join the fiscal fray
For my docks and slipways,
Boats and ships,
And none shall say me nay!

Railway shareholders
Paddington to Temple Meads –
London Town to Bristol.
Streaming steam and racing wheels –
Shrill and distant whistle.
>   Temple Meads – Temple Meads
>   Paddington to Temple Meads.
>   Streaming steam and racing wheels –
Shrill and distant whistle.

Bristol Men:
Oh, Bristol Men
Are business men
And Bristol Men are canny.
We drive a bargain to the hilt
And value every penny.
>   Bristol Men -
>   Bristol Men –
You don't bamboozle Bristol Men,
For Bristol Men
Are business men
And careful of their money!

London Men
Oh, London Men
Are prideful men,
>   And London Men are lofty.
>   We are not men as others are,
>   We give our orders softly.
>   London Men –
>   London Men
You can't outwit us London Men;
We are not men as others are,
We give our orders softly.

Paddington to Temple Meads –
London Town to Bristol.
Streaming steam and racing wheels –
Shrill and distant whistle.
> Temple Meads – Temple Meads
> Paddington to Temple Meads.
> Streaming steam and racing wheels –
Shrill and distant whistle.

Box Tunnel

Dead Men
We are the ghosts of Box.
We are the tunnelling men.
One hundred of us
We never came home –
Walked in the Tunnel
But never came home...
Never came out of Box,
      Box Tunnel.

Down in the thick and sulph'rous air,
Down where a thousand candles glare
In stinking mud
In murk and gloom
With pounding pumps
With rock-fall boom
With gunpowder blast
Like the crack of doom...
      We laid us down in Box Tunnel.
      Box Tunnel
        Our tomb.

When your train runs under Box Hill
We are there – the tunnelling men.
You may glimpse our shades on the Tunnel wall
Or catch our echoing, dying call
Box laid us low, who once stood tall
The tunnelling men of Box...
      Box Tunnel.

Train upholstery women
When you're sitting on your seat
Upon your sit-upon,
As the locomotive races down the line;
When you're comfortably bolstered
And cosily upholstered,
When you're travelling at speed
And feeling fine.

When you're sitting on your seat
Upon your sit-upon,
When you're full of cheer and just about to dine;
Spare a thought for all of those,
Who have cushioned your repose -
Swindon women...
   Swindon women...
         As the locomotive races down the line!

We stitch and sew,
With needle and yarn,
We tack and baste and pin.
We stuff and wad,
We button and pipe,
We snip and clip and trim.

   Upholstery women's nimble hands
   Make sure you sit at ease −
   Padded and pillowed,
   Curtained and draped,
   As pretty as you please.

When you're sitting on your seat
Upon your sit-upon,
As the locomotive races down the line;
When you're comfortably bolstered
And cosily upholstered,
When you're travelling at speed
And feeling fine.

When you're sitting on your seat
Upon your sit-upon,
When you're full of cheer and just about to dine;
Spare a thought for all of those,
Who have cushioned your repose -
Swindon women...
   Swindon women...
       As the locomotive races down the line!

  Train assembly workers
  Noise! Noise! Noise! (*ad lib*)
  Full blast! Bone-shatter! Ear-split smash!
  Swelling and bellowing, clamouring clash!
  Fills our heads with its thunderous crash!
  Pandemonium! Pandemonium!
       That's... The Noise!

  Oh, the hammers ram
  To the furnace roar
  As the sparks rain down
  On the foundry floor,
  And our ears are deaf
  And our mouths are dumb
     It's the Noise -
     The Noise –
  A Noise like Kingdom Come!

IKB, dying
No… more… 'En Avent'…
Born of my brain,
My loved ones,
My children –
Great Bridge and Great Ship,
Created by me.
With travail and pain
I brought to fruition
The fruit of my brain
On the land and the sea.

Across the Tamar,
Loop and tube,
My Serpent Bridge
Displays its coils;
While down the Severn
My Giant Ship
Has slipped her chains,
Escaped their toils…….

I'll cross my Bridge,
I'll sail my Ship,
Till I… at last…
Escape… life's… toils…………..

THE MAGIC
FISHBONE

from **THE MAGIC FISHBONE**
based on a short story by Charles Dickens

Written in collaboration with Graham Lines.
First performance by the Longlea Singers 2012

In the far-off land of Watkinsonia, King Watkins struggles to support his family and pay his bills. Will the arrival of Fairy Grandmarina solve his problems?

Sunshiny Day / Rise and Shine

Princess Alicia Watkins
Oh, it's…
Such a sunshiny day!
A skylarking, sunshiny day!
I feel I could cartwheel right up into space –
Go kicking my heels up all over the place –
For the sunshine has painted a smile on my face
On this sparkling, sunshiny day!

For…   The sun has polished his buttons,
       The trees are tapping their feet.
       And every bird
       That ever was heard
       Is twittering, 'tweet, tweet, tweet'.
And… The sky is blueing his laundry,
       The west wind whistles his song;
       And every cloud
       All fluffy and proud
       Is puff, puff, puffing along.

For, it's…
Such a sunshiny day!
A skylarking, sunshiny day!
I feel I could cartwheel right up into space –
Go kicking my heels up all over the place –
For the sunshine has painted a smile on my face
On this windy and wonderful,
Gleaming and glorious,
Sparkling sunshiny day!

Loyal Watkinsonians
Rise and shine! / That's the way of it.
Rise and Shine! / Every day a bit
Harder to get out of bed / Stack our veg or bake our bread.
Harder still to earn a crust / Now the Royal Bank is bust.
Rise and Shine! / Till we're sick of it.
Rise and Shine! / That's the tricky bit.
Early rising's not our dish / Grinding sausage, scaling fish.
Rheumatis and aching knees / Aggravate our miseries.
Profits plummet,
Payment's late,
Everything is on the slate…
How are we to operate?
Let alone
RISE… AND… SHINE!

(*Royal babies, off*)
WAAAAAAH! WAAAAAAH!

I Loves Fish

Fishmonger's Boy
I - LOVES – FISH! It's my favourite dish.
At every meal, I only wish to see before me on a dish
Hot and savoury and delish... Fish! Fish! Fish!

Whatever the catch that the fishermen make,
Be it scallops or clams, be it sardines or hake,
If it's fish you can simmer or griddle or bake...
     Fish is the dish for me!

No matter what manner of species they get,
So long as it's shelly, or scaly and wet,
Whether caught by a fish-trap, a line or a net...
     Fish is the dish for me!

Oh, the herring and the brill,
The mackerel and the eel,
The lobster and the oyster and the flounder.
Oh, the turbot and the plaice,
The halibut and the dace,
The winkle and the cockle and the conger.
     For the garfish and the bass
     The darfish and the wrasse,
My piscatorial love could not be stronger:
     But the King of all the fish...
     The fish for which I wish...
Is the Salmon, Royal Salmon, priceless Salmon...
That's the fish for this fishmo...ong...er!

Whatever is caught in a fisherman's trawl,
Should it swim or sit tight, should it scuttle or crawl,
Be it catfish or dogfish which comes when you call...
     Fish is the dish for me!

Whatever appears on the fishmonger's slab,
The tunny, the pilchard, the sole or the dab,
The predator pike or the counterfeit crab...
      Fish is the dish for me!
Oh, the herring and the brill,
The mackerel and the eel,
The lobster and the oyster and the flounder.
Oh, the turbot and the plaice,
The halibut and the dace,
The winkle and the cockle and the conger.
      For the garfish and the bass
      The darfish and the wrasse,
My piscatorial love could not be stronger:
      But the King of all the fish...
      The fish for which I wish...
Is the Salmon, Royal Salmon, priceless Salmon...

Yes, Salmon's the King of them all!

Calculating Fiend

The Chancellor
Any criminal who chortles at the guilty deed he's done
       Wouldn't think it worth a fig if only multiplied by **1**
But there's nothing more delightful to a ruthless thugeroo
       Than some pitiless chicanery that's multiplied by **2**.
There's nothing more exalting to a stinker than a spree
       Of unashamed wickedness that multiplied by **3**
And proper-minded scoundrels will admit they just adore
       Any evil hanky-panky which is multiplied by **4**
While there's not a single diabolic scallywag alive
       Who wouldn't jump at multiplying treachery by **5**.

       Oooo... I'm... a...
       Calculating fiend!
       A calculating fiend!
       I'm multiplied malevolence,
       A calculating fiend!

The dedicated blackguards who indulge in dirty tricks
       Are pleased as punch to find that they are multiplied by **6**,
And your monsters of iniquity consider they're in heaven
       If their knavery and treason can be multiplied by **7**.
While crooks and cons and swindlers will all congratulate
       Each other when their felonies are multiplied by **8**.
So if ever you should come across a racketeering swine
       You can bet your boots his villanies are multiplied by **9**...
BUT...The sweetest taste by far to ME – most dastardly of men,
Is a dish of Cold Revenge... when it's been multiplied by **10**!

       Oooo... I'm... a...
       Calculating fiend!
       A calculating fiend!
       I'm multiplied malevolence,
       A calculating fiend!

A Little Machine To Do It

King Watkins (at the counting house)
I wish there was a little machine to do it;
To spell and add and difficult things like that.
I wish there was a sort of a calcu-wottsit,
With all of the answers certain to come out pat...
      Maybe if you pressed a button or something?

I wish there was a sort of a grand contraption,
To take me back and forth on a comfy seat;
With wheels that never needed my legs to drive 'em,
And save my poor old bottom and aching feet.

I wish there was a hole-in-the-wall for money,
To dole out all the guineas that I require.
I wish my land was flowing with milk and honey...
And closer to the dream of my heart's desire.

      Wishing is free, (I'm glad to say),
      That's why I wish and dream all day.
      Wishing is one thing I can do
      That costs me nothing and might come true...

I wish there was a powerful sort of engine
With wings and things to carry me through the air.
A staircase moving upwards and never ending -
      A clever device, a gimmicky-dodge,
      A nickery-nackery thingamabobbery
Little machine to get me out of here!

Have a salmon for your supper

The Fairy Grandmarina
Attend to what I say,
Don't sigh and look away,
It's most important we
Should rapidly agree.
So concentrate and give me your attention,
And everything will work out to perfection!

Have a salmon for your supper or your dinner or your tea,
(Having bought the finest sample of this monarch of the sea);
Have it cooked without delay and partake this very day,
Making sure that you prepare it in the way that I shall say.
Disregarding protestations that the fish is liverish,
Have the choicest of the salmon put upon your daughter's dish…
(*dramatic pause*)
And when she finds the WISHBONE
In the semblance of a FISHBONE…
Let her clean and rub-a-dub it, let her polish it and scrub it,
Let her cherish it and keep it, let her lovingly secrete it,
Let her guard its magic power till she senses it's the hour
When she's absolutely, positively certain
That it's time to make her WISH!

Ultimatum Time!

Shopkeepers
It's Ultimatum… Time!
We are here to get our dues.
Full Compensa…tion Time
And we're tightening the screws!
We want our owings paid,
Full restitution made.
It's Ultima… tum Time
For the Royals!

Chancellor (oily)
Why be hasty?
Don't be hard.
Mercy brings
Its own reward.
Try to see things from King Watkins point of view…
Fatherhood has knocked his budget black and blue.
All those children,
(What a brood!)
All those nappies,
All that food –
He would pay you if he could.
Why be hasty?

Shopkeepers
It's Ultima… tum Time!
We have suffered long enough,
It's Retribu… tion Time,
Time to take him by the scruff.
Watkins' credit's up the spout,
Time to call the bailiffs out!

Chancellor
Why be hasty,
Pause a while.
Try your best
To raise a smile.
After all it's
Only *money* that he owes.
Who's the winner if
You *force* me to foreclose?
In a year or
Three or four…
Five or six
(Or maybe more),
He'd be *bound* to pay his score –
Why be hasty?

Last Day in the Dear Old Palace

Queen Watkins and Royal Children
It's our last day
In the dear old Palace,
Last day in our home.
Goodbye our cosy kitchen,
Spicy, sweet and hot;
Sugar crock and cookie jar,
Kettle, pan and pot.
You may be old and battered
But you'll never be forgot...
When we think of this day –
The very last day in our home.

We have packed our bags and we've bundled our belonging,
Now we can't hold back the lamenting and the longings
For the home we love – snatched and sold off without warning...
Time for tears...
Time for mourning...

It's our last day
In the dear old Palace,
Last day in our home.
Goodbye, beloved nursery,
Cradle, crib and cot;
Nursing-chair and rocking-horse,
Basin, jug and pot.
You may be chipped and shabby
But you'll never be forgot...
When we think of this day –
The very last day
In our home......

Acknowledgements

Many thanks to: Music Sales Ltd, Betty Roe MBE, the late John Bishop, Carol Bishop, Graham Lines, Rosalind Roland, Anna Lines, June and Christopher Keyte, Janice Thompson, Marjorie Bruce, Suzanne Walker, Gillian Wormley, Soo Bishop, the late Elizabeth Connell, Graham Trew, David Johnston, Barry Collett, Ronald Corp, Graham Pullin, Jill Meagre.

Cover illustration by Dylan Stone, copyright 2012